What Is a Family?

A Catechism for Diagnosing and Restoring the Christian Home

SCOTT T. BROWN

Church & Family Life
Wake Forest, NC

What Is a Family? A Catechism for Diagnosing and Restoring the Christian Home

First Printing: February 2026

Church & Family Life
220 South White St., Wake Forest, NC 27587
www.churchandfamilylife.com

ISBN: 978-1-62418-077-4

Cover Design and Typography by Turley and Sons Design Co.

Printed in the United States of America.

Endorsements

With brevity, clarity, and biblical faithfulness, my dear friend Scott Brown has bequeathed to the church this well-crafted, valuable synopsis of family life, marriage, manhood, womanhood, childrearing, and family worship from a Reformed perspective. Read this catechism. Pray over it. Weep over it. Teach it to your children, line upon line. And above all, live its truths for the glory of the Father who has adopted us into His family, and the Son who has betrothed us to Himself forever. A radical return to the beautiful, refreshing model for family life outlined in Scripture is the crying need of our day in the family, the church, and the nation.

—Dr. Joel R. Beeke, chancellor of Puritan Reformed Theological Seminary, and pastor of Heritage Reformed Congregation, Grand Rapids, Michigan

The family is central to virtually every societal endeavor under God: from education (Prov. 22:6) to charity (1 Tim. 5:8), from economics (Deut. 21:17) to individual discipleship (Eph. 6:1-4), from the care of the aged (1 Tim. 5:3-13) to the subduing of the earth (Gen. 1:26-28). This catechism is a primer for all these things and more. Highly recommended.

—George Grant, pastor of Parish Presbyterian Church, Franklin, Tennessee

Scott Brown is at it again! In this *Catechism on the Family,* he has a found a new way to remind us all and to teach our children basic, biblical truths about the family. This is so important in a day when such basic, biblical truths are being buried in an avalanche of silly, woke wickedness. May God bless his labors!

—Sam Waldron, dean and professor of Systematic Theology at Covenant Baptist Theological Seminary, and author of *A Man as Priest in His Home*

In a deeply confused age, this catechism shines the light of Scripture into the darkness. This God-given tool will strengthen your family and reorient it according to God's design. What is a God-defined family? What is godly manhood? What is virtuous womanhood? *A Catechism on the Family* answers 201 questions with God's infallible Word. Delivered with conviction and clarity, these answers are accessible, memorable, and Christ-honoring.

—Jeff Pollard, editor of the *Free Grace Broadcaster* and retired pastor of Mt. Zion Bible Church

A Catechism on the Family is a remarkably rich and concise resource. In just a few pages, it delivers a robust, theologically grounded summary of the biblical doctrine of the family. Every sentence is saturated with truth, touching on virtually every facet of family life through the lens of Scripture. It powerfully affirms the beauty and significance of the family in God's design and redemptive purposes. Clearly the fruit of deep study and long ministry experience, this work leaves no stone unturned. I can easily see myself using it in every pre-marital counseling session—both as a study tool and as a foundation for shared conviction. This is an invaluable resource for individuals, couples, and churches alike.

—Jeffrey Johnson, pastor of Grace Bible Church, Conway, Arkansas, president of Grace Bible Theological Seminary, and founder of Free Grace Press

Scott Brown's catechism provides sound biblical theology on men, women, and the family, along with relevant Scripture references, that will aid parents training children and pastors seeking to teach these important truths to their congregations. Catechisms are time-tested tools for teaching theology, and there are few topics as important in our day as that of the family. I highly commend this work and plan to use it in my own teaching.

—Zachary Garris, pastor of Bryce Avenue Presbyterian Church (PCA), White Rock, New Mexico

If we want to learn to live well in God's world we must recover what He has revealed about the family and begin to reorder our lives accordingly. Scott Brown has provided an excellent resource to assist in doing just that. Foundational truths that previous generations of Western Civilization could take for granted have been so eroded over the last two hundred years that modern Christians can often be disoriented, confused, and intimidated regarding how to follow Christ in day-to-day life. One of the most crucial of those truths is the nature and purpose of the family. God created the family and He did so before He created the church or the state. This catechism on the family asks basic questions related to the nature and work of this God-ordained institution and then provides simple answers from God's Word. In addition, each section includes helpful questions for reflection and suggestions for fathers as they teach these vital truths in their homes. This book will help moms and dads understand more clearly what God intends for them to be and do as they seek to fulfill the high calling He has given to them to pursue in the home. Single adults, church officers, and children will also find a wealth of biblical guidance here as they fulfill their respective responsibilities to the Lord. Use this book to help recover the priority of the family in the world.

—Tom Ascol, pastor at Grace Baptist Church, and president of Founders Ministries, Cape Coral, Florida

Written in the style of the historic Christian catechisms that have proven to be so helpful to the people of God, Scott Brown's *Catechism on the Family* is sure to follow suit. This compass of biblical truth on the family will bless anyone who is willing to study its contents; and in a day where we have witnessed such a massive breakdown of the biblical family, a resource such as this will most definitely help to repair the ruins. I pray that it receives a wide reading and that the Lord will bless it to many souls.

—Kyle Reeder, pastor of The Solid Rock Baptist Church, Benton, Kentucky

This catechism is dedicated
to my pastor in my teens
and twenties, John Tebay,
who taught me the rare
fundamentals of family life,
church life, and expository
preaching in the earliest days
of my Christian walk.

Acknowledgments

I'm very grateful for the men who reviewed this catechism and offered valuable feedback: Jeffrey Johnson, Dr. Joel Beeke, Jeff Pollard, Tom Ascol, Dr. George Grant, Zachary Garris, Sam Waldron, and last but not least, Kyle Reeder, who encouraged me to do it in the first place. Special thanks to Wesley Strackbein who provided constant vigilance in proofreading and editing through many revisions.

Table of Contents

For a New Generation of Families

There are moments in history when a people forget who they are and what they ought to do. This is what has happened with family life in America.

In the last century—and in this one still—the church has largely traded the scriptural pattern for what a family is for a newer, shinier script written by the spirit of the age.

This period will go down in history as a bad time for the family in America. Looking back on this era, wise observers will see that the biblical doctrine of the family, and the biblical functionality of the family, were forgotten by most and nearly obliterated—even among Christians.

It is time to recover the lost biblical patterns and reclaim what God designed a family to be.

That is the purpose of this catechism.

A new generation must be taught again what their parents and grandparents missed. This is critical because many of the great maladies of our culture can be traced back to biblically ignorant and even dysfunctional families. It has been said many times: as the family goes, so goes the church; as the church goes, so goes the culture. This is more than a catchy phrase; our culture today is in ruins because we've spurned God's vision for family life.

The well-being of the world depends on the preservation of the Gospel from one generation to the next. God has given this treasure to families and churches to pass on. Each generation must begin afresh, and the pattern of godliness must continue or the succeeding generations will be lost in darkness. This is why God lays a great calling on every generation to be a blessing to the rising generations by doing their duty in their families.

It's time to dust off the old doctrine, revive it, and put it into practice. A new generation needs a firm foundation to build their families upon.

This catechism is designed as a blueprint for a new generation who refuse to let God's design for the home be forgotten. It reclaims Scripture's teaching on marriage, parenting, household order, and generational legacy—with clarity, conviction, and courage. Each section contains helpful questions for discussion with your family.

My hope for this tool is that it would help parents and church members to give themselves entirely to God to care for the next generation; to saturate their homes with the Gospel of Jesus Christ; to create a home life that serves as a nursery for the church and the nation; to educate their children in the Word of God; and to create a family life that conforms to the biblical vision; to work in such a way, everyday, so that the members of that family can say, "Our home was a little piece of heaven."

All of this for the spread of the Gospel and the well-being of families in the church for many generations.

Let us rise to the task and repair the family, fuel the church, and shape future generations! Let's mend what has been broken, strengthen what remains, and plant what may yet flourish. The future, after all, is not an enemy to be feared but a field to be sown. And God has placed this generation precisely where it is, at precisely this hour, for precisely this work.

You were born for this moment—so, arise and build! Take up the task with courage.

Let the world see what happens when a new generation stands on the firm foundation of God's sufficient Word.

> *And they shall rebuild the old ruins,*
> *They shall raise up the former desolations,*
> *And they shall repair the ruined cities,*
> *The desolations of many generations.—Isa. 61:4*

Scott Brown
Wake Forest, NC
February 2026

Men and Women: Created in God's Image for Different Roles

Equal Worth, Distinct Roles

1 **Q:** *Who created man and woman?*

A: God (Gen. 1:27; 2:7, 21-22).

2 **Q:** *How did God create man and woman?*

A: God formed Adam first, as man and ruler, from the dust of the ground; and Eve, second, as woman and helper from Adam's rib, creating both in His own image (Gen. 1:27; 2:7, 21-23).

3 **Q:** *Are men and women created equal?*

A: Men and women are both created in God's image and are equally valuable in His sight (Gen. 1:27; Gal. 3:28-29).

4 **Q:** *Are men and women created different?*

A: God created men and women in His own image, yet different, making them distinctly male and female, by nature, and giving them unique roles specific to their nature (Gen. 1:27; 2:7, 18, 21-23; 3:16-20; 5:1-2; Eph. 5:22-33; 1 Cor. 11:3; Prov. 31:10-31).

REFLECTION

God made both men and women in His image, equal in worth, yet distinct in role. These differences are not flaws but gifts, designed by a wise and loving Creator. Do we rejoice in the differences between men and women, and trust that God knows what is best for human flourishing?

Help for Parents: Read *Genesis 1:27* aloud. Invite each child to name one way they see God's goodness in how men and women complement each other (strengths, perspectives, roles). Close in prayer, thanking God that His design is both wise and good.

Embracing God's Design

5 **Q:** What are the differences between men and women?

A: Men and women are fundamentally different in their creation order roles, being made for separate and distinct duties under God's authority (Gen. 3:16-20; 1 Cor. 11:3, 8-9; Eph. 5:22-33; 1 Tim. 2:11-15; Deut. 1:13).

6 **Q:** What is a man?

A: A man is a fixed biologically male person, uniquely created by God in His image; originally very good, but sinful by the Fall; created to rule; as married, to be the covenant head of his wife and family, leading them with grace, mercy, wisdom and love in a godly dominion mission; and, as a husband, called to be the living symbol of Christ's love for His church (Gen. 1:27-28; 1:31; 3:1-19; Rom. 5:12; 1 Cor. 11:3, 8-9; Eph. 5:23-28, 31-33).

7 **Q:** What is a woman?

A: A woman is a fixed biologically female person, uniquely created from the man by God in His image; originally very good, but sinful by the Fall; as married, designed to be man's suitable and submissive helper; to conceive, bear, nurse and nurture children; to be man's coregent in having dominion over the earth; and called to be the living symbol of Christ's church (Gen. 1:27-28; 1:31; 2:18, 21-24; 3:1-19; 1 Cor. 11:3, 8-9; Gen. 3:16, 20; 24:60; Ps. 113:9; 128:3; Isa. 49:15; Eph. 5:22-25).

8 **Q:** Can men and women choose their sex?

A: Men and women cannot choose their sex for, following Adam and Eve's creation, it is established by God as either male or female at the moment of conception (Gen. 1:27; Ps. 139:14-17; Jer. 1:5).

9 **Q:** How should Christians view a person who claims to be a different sex than the one God assigned at conception?

A: According to God's Word, it should be seen as defiance against God and a deluded perversion of His created order (Gen. 1:27; Ps. 139:14-16; Rom. 9:20; 1:19-28).

10 **Q:** How should Christians view sodomite[1] attraction, as well as sexual activity with those of the same sex?

A: According to God's Word, it should be seen as defiance against God and an abominable perversion of His created order, which defiles the land and invites His solemn judgment (Rom. 1:19-28; 1 Cor. 6:9-10; 1 Tim. 1:8-11; Jude 7; Lev. 18:22-30; 20:13).

REFLECTION

The sex with which we are born is not ours to choose; it is God's gift at conception. To deny or distort this is to stand in open rebellion against the Creator. Scripture speaks of same-sex attraction and practice as abominable, a rejection of His order that invites judgment. Do we bow our knees before

1. **sodomite** - a man or woman who, in defiance of God's established order, has unseemly physical intercourse with someone of the same sex, as occurred in the city of Sodom before God destroyed it (Rom. 1:25-27; Gen. 19:1-29).

God's wisdom, or do we try to sit in judgment over His design?

Help for Parents: Read *Romans 1:22–27*. With older children, discuss how the culture celebrates what God condemns, and why faithfulness to Scripture may be costly. With younger children, emphasize: "God made boys to be boys, and girls to be girls, and that is very good." Pray for courage to stand firm and compassion to speak the truth in love.

The Value of Human Life

11 **Q:** Why is human life sacred?

A: Because humans, both male and female, are created in God's image (Gen. 1:27; 5:1-2; James 3:9).

12 **Q:** How were men and women created in God's image?

A: God created male and female in His own image, in knowledge, righteousness, holiness, and dominion (Col. 3:10; Eph. 4:24; Gen. 1:26-28; Ps. 8:3-8).

13 **Q:** Why do men and women bear God's image?

A: For several reasons:

- To worship God and give Him glory as His earthly image-bearers (Ps. 29:2; 95:6; 103:1; 105:3; 115:1; Isa. 25:1; 1 Cor. 6:19-20; 10:31);
- To show forth the communicable attributes of God they possess (Gal. 5:22-24; Eph. 5:1-2; 1 Pet. 1:15-16; 1 John 4:19);
- To reflect God's perfect rule, as stewards, by taking dominion over the earth (Gen. 1:26-28; Ps. 8:3-8).

14 **Q:** How are men and women different from animals?

A: Unlike animals, God endowed men and women with living, reasonable, and immortal souls, having the law of God written in their hearts with power to fulfill it, yet subject to fall (Gen. 1:27; 2:7; 3:6; Job 35:11; Eccles. 12:7; Matt. 10:28; Luke 23:43; Rom. 2:14-15; Eccles. 7:29).

15 **Q:** When does human life begin?

A: At the moment of conception (Ps. 139:13-16; Isa. 44:2; Eccles. 11:5).

16 **Q:** Who forms children in the womb?

A: Although He uses the human act of procreation,[2] God forms children in the womb, fearfully and

2. **procreation** – the physical act of union between man and woman that brings forth children, whenever God opens the womb.

wonderfully creating them in His image (Gen. 4:1; Ps. 139:13-16; Isa. 44:2; Jer. 1:5; Eccles. 11:5; Ps. 127:3; Gen. 1:27).

17 **Q:** Why is abortion evil?

A: Because it is the murder of an unborn child who is made in God's image (Gen. 1:27; Ps. 139:13-16; Exod. 20:13).

18 **Q:** Why did God institute capital punishment for murder after the Flood?

A: Because man is made in God's image, life is sacred, and those who murder their fellow man must pay the punishment with their life (Gen. 1:27; 9:6; Exod. 21:12; Lev. 24:17; Num. 35:30-31).

REFLECTION

Every human life bears God's image, from the unborn child to elderly grandparents. Life is sacred because it reflects God Himself. How should this truth shape the way we speak, care, and act toward others?

Help for Parents: Read *Psalm 139:13–16.* Thank God aloud for each family member. Then pray for unborn children, for parents in difficult circumstances, and for God's mercy to protect life.

Order in the Home, Church, and Society

19 **Q:** Why are men given the responsibility to rule?

A: Man was created first as God's direct earthly representative, whereas the woman, created second, derives her origin from man, was created for man, and was deceived at the Fall (Gen. 2:15, 18-22; 1 Cor. 11:3, 8-9; 1 Tim. 2:11-14).

20 **Q:** In what key realms do the roles of men and women differ?

A: God has ordained the roles of men and women to be distinct within the family, the church, and the state (Eph. 5:22-33; 1 Tim. 2:11-15; Deut. 1:13).

21 **Q:** How are men's and women's roles distinct within the family?

A: A husband is to be the head of his wife, and what children the sovereign Lord puts in his care, with his wife respectfully submitting to him as his helper (Eph. 5:22-33; Col. 3:18-19; Gen. 2:18; Eph. 6:4; Prov. 4:1).

22 **Q:** How are men's and women's roles distinct within the church?

A: As with the Old Testament priesthood, men are to

exclusively rule as elders and serve as deacons in the church (Lev. 7:34-36; Num. 18:1-7; 1 Tim. 3:1-13; Titus 1:5-9; 1 Tim. 2:11-15).

23 **Q:** How are men's and women's roles distinct within the state?

A: Men, not women, are ordained by God to function as civil rulers (Exod. 18:21-22; Deut. 1:13; 17:15; Prov. 20:8, 18; Rom. 13:1-4).

24 **Q:** Considering God's established order for civil government, how does one account for Deborah's service as a judge?

A: Deborah's singular and peculiar example, during a time of judgment and disorder, does not negate God's prescriptive commands for men to serve as civil rulers (Judg. 4; Exod. 18:21-22; Deut. 1:13; Isa. 3:1-5, 11-12).

REFLECTION

God has ordained men to bear the weight of leadership in the home, the church, and society. This is not tyranny but stewardship; not privilege but responsibility. When we reject this order, chaos and judgment follow. Do we gladly embrace God's order, or do we resist His wisdom?

Help for Parents: Read *Ephesians 5:22–33.* Fathers: confess any failures in loving leadership, repent before your family, and pray that the Lord will grant you grace to overcome your failures. Wives and children: share one way you can encourage or support the father's leadership. Pray together for your home to reflect Christ's pattern of love and honor.

Family Discussion

For Fathers to Ask at the Table

1. If men and women are equally made in God's image, why do you think God gave them different roles?
2. How does understanding God's design for men and women help us resist the confusion in our culture about gender and identity?
3. What does it mean for our family that men and women are called to serve together as co-regents under God?

For Children (Simpler Prompts)

1. Who made boys and girls?
2. Are boys and girls the same or different? How?
3. How can we honor God with the way He made us?

Try This Tonight

Read *Genesis 1:26–28* and *Ephesians 5:22–33* together. Then ask each family member to thank God out loud for one way He made them, whether as male or female. Close by praying that God would help each of you live joyfully in the role He has given.

Memory Verse

> *"So God created man in His own image; in the image of God He created him; male and female He created them."—Genesis 1:27*

Hymn

"All Creatures of Our God and King"

Marriage and Family: Created by God

The First Institution

25 **Q:** What is the first human institution established by God in history?

A: The family (Gen. 1:26-28; 2:18-25).

26 **Q:** What other human institutions did God establish later on?

A: The church and the state (Matt. 16:15-18; 28:18-20; Acts 2:40-42; Gen. 9:6; Rom. 13:1-3; 1 Pet. 2:13-15).

27 **Q:** How did God establish the family?

A: God established the family as the final act of creation week when he brought Adam and Eve together in marriage (Gen. 1:26-28; 2:18-25).

28 **Q:** Was the first family also the first church?

A: Likely, yes. In their worship and fellowship with God, Adam and Eve were also the first gathering of

His people—the beginning of the church (Gen. 3:15; 4:1-5).[1]

REFLECTION

Why did God start with the family instead of the church or the state? What does that tell us about its importance?

Help for Parents: Use this as a chance to remind your children: "Our family was God's idea. We belong to Him." Encourage each child to share one blessing of being part of your family.

God's Ownership

29 **Q:** To whom does the family belong?

A: The family is God's sacred institution and is not a creation of the state or church or an invention of man (Gen. 1:26-28; 2:18-25; Mal. 2:11; Matt. 19:4-6).

30 **Q:** How is a new family formed?

A: A new family is formed when a man and woman

1. Puritans such as John Owen and William Ames maintained that the church began after the Fall, when God preached the first Gospel message to Adam and Eve, and they began to offer sacrifices of worship with their family (Gen. 3:15; 4:1-7).

are lawfully joined together in marriage, by oath,[2] in a one-flesh covenant[3] (Gen. 2:22-24; Matt. 19:4-6; Mal. 2:14).

REFLECTION

The family is not man's invention. How should that truth shape the way we treat family roles and responsibilities?

Help for Parents: Lead the family in saying together: "Our family belongs to God." Then pray together that your home would reflect His design.

What Is a Family?

31 **Q:** What does a family consist of?

A: A family consists of a man, the husband, and a woman, the wife, and their children, including those fostered or adopted (Gen. 1:27-28; 2:18-24; 4:1; Ps. 128; 2 Cor. 6:18; 1 John 3:1).

2. **oath** – a solemn affirmation or declaration, made with an appeal to God for the truth of what is affirmed.

3. **one-flesh covenant** – a solemn agreement between husband and wife, made before God, to be joined physically, spiritually, and relationally in unity.

32 **Q:** What is marriage?

A: Marriage is a holy institution, ordained by God, in which a man and woman are joined together as husband and wife, by oath, in a one-flesh covenant, until death separates them (Gen. 2:21-24; Mal. 2:11, 14; Matt. 19:4-6; Heb. 13:4; Rom. 7:2-3; 1 Cor. 7:39).

REFLECTION

In today's culture, "family" can be defined many different ways. How does God define it? Why does His definition matter more than popular opinion?

Help for Parents: Write "God's Design" at the top of a sheet of paper, and have your kids list what God says makes up a family. Post it somewhere in the house as a reminder.

The Covenant of Marriage

33 **Q:** Why is a covenant so integral to the creation of a lawful marriage?

A: It establishes the binding nature of marriage, not as a mere contract which can be easily broken or dissolved, but as an oath-bound commitment which reflects God's character as One who always keeps covenant with His people (Mal. 2:14; Prov. 2:17; Ps. 15:4; Mark 10:7-9; Ezek. 16:8; Deut. 7:9; Ps. 89:34).

REFLECTION

Why is a covenant stronger than a contract? How does this show us something about God's love?

Help for Parents: If you're married, briefly share your wedding story with your kids and how you made a covenant before God. If your children are older, ask them what they think a covenant commitment means.

The Purpose of Marriage

34 **Q:** What does marriage accomplish?

A: It creates an independent new government with the man and woman leaving their fathers' house and cleaving to one another (Gen. 2:23-24; Mark 10:6-8).

35 **Q:** Why did God create marriage?

A: God created marriage:

- For mankind to take dominion over God's creation (Gen. 1:26-28; 2:15, 19-20; Ps. 8:4-8; 115:16);
- For companionship for the man and the woman (Gen 2:18, 23; 1 Pet. 3:7);
- For the increase of mankind through procreation (Gen. 1:28; 9:1, 7; Mal. 2:15);

- So that the natural desire of men and women for intimacy would be directed in all purity (Prov. 5:18-19; 1 Cor. 7:2, 9; Heb. 13:4);
- For protection from the devastating effects of immorality so that the land might not be defiled (Jer. 3:1-2, 9; Lev. 18:20-29);
- For bringing up children in the training and admonition of the Lord (Deut. 6:1-9; Prov. 4:1-4; 22:6; Isa. 38:19; Eph. 6:1-4);
- For picturing the Gospel of Jesus Christ to the world (Eph. 5:22-32).

REFLECTION

God gave marriage many purposes: companionship, children, purity, dominion, and the picture of Christ and His church. Which one do you think your family reflects best right now? Which one needs the most growth?

Help for Parents: Choose one of these purposes as a "focus of the week." For example, if it's companionship, plan a small family outing together and talk about God's gift of companionship.

Purity, Adultery, Divorce

36 **Q.** What is the nature of the sexual relationship?

A. The marriage bed of husband and wife is sacred and should be kept undefiled by adultery (Exod. 20:14; Matt. 5:27-28; Heb. 13:4).

37 **Q.** What is adultery?

A. The willful and voluntary violation of the marriage bed, committed between a married person and someone other than that person's current husband or wife (Exod. 20:14; Deut. 22:22: Prov. 6:29; Heb. 13:4).

38 **Q.** How does God view adultery?

A. As a wicked act, in violation of His express law given in the Seventh Commandment, which destroys families and invites His solemn judgment (Exod. 20:14; Deut. 5:18; Prov. 6:20-35; Jer. 5:8-9).

39 **Q.** How does God view marital divorce?

A. He hates it (Mal. 2:16).

40 **Q.** Is it ever lawful for a man and woman to divorce?

A. Only when adultery has been committed, or one has been abandoned by their spouse, can the innocent party lawfully pursue a divorce (Matt. 5:31-32; 19:6-9; 1 Cor. 7:15).

REFLECTION

Why does God take faithfulness in marriage so seriously? How does our family show loyalty and love to one another?

Help for Parents: For younger kids, illustrate faithfulness with something simple (like keeping promises). For older kids, talk candidly about how sin harms families and how God protects us through His commands.

Family Discussion

For Fathers to Ask at the Table

1. Why do you think God made the family the first institution?
2. How does knowing that marriage is a covenant (not just a contract) change the way we should think about promises?
3. In what ways can our family "take dominion" for God's glory right here in our home, neighborhood, or church?

For Children (Simpler Prompts)

1. What is a family?
2. Who thought of marriage first—God or people?
3. How can we show that our family belongs to God?

Try This Tonight

Read Genesis *2:18–25* aloud. Then have each child share one way they see God's goodness in creating families. Close by praying that God would help your family live in a way that honors Him.

Memory Verse

> *"Therefore a man shall leave his father and mother and be joined to his wife, and they shall become one flesh."—Genesis 2:24*

Hymn

"O Father, All Creating"

The Family: Builder and Caretaker of the Earth

God's Dominion Mandate

41 **Q.** To whom was the Dominion Mandate given?

A. God gave it to man and his wife—not to angels, animals, or any other creature (Gen. 1:26-28; 2:15; 19-20; Ps. 8:4-8).

42 **Q.** What does the Dominion Mandate mean?

A. As the first married couple, Adam and Eve were called to "Be fruitful and multiply; fill the earth and subdue it; have dominion over the fish of the sea, over the birds of the air, and over every living thing that moves on the earth" (Gen. 1:28).

REFLECTION

God entrusted the care of the earth not to angels, animals, or governments, but to His image bearers. This gives families and individuals daily work and household life eternal significance. Do we see our ourselves as participants in God's great dominion mission?

Help for Parents: Read *Genesis 1:28*. Brainstorm one small way your family can better steward what God has given—it could be caring for your yard, managing finances wisely, or reaching out to neighbors. Choose one to practice this week.

The Family as Economic & Cultural Force

43 **Q.** What does the Dominion Mandate tell us about the family?

A. That the family, God's first institution, and all God's image-bearers consequently (including singles), were given primacy in taking dominion and should take the lead as an economic and cultural force (Gen. 1:26-28; 4:20-22; 9:1, 7; Ps. 8:3-8).

44 **Q.** When it comes to the family, how should one's home and property relate to the Dominion Mandate?

A. Upon marrying, a husband and wife should actively make the most of the property under their stewardship (Prov. 14:1; 27:23; 31:10, 27; Jer. 29:5-7; Titus 2:3-5).

45 **Q.** How should a husband and wife steward what God has given them?

A. With prayer, wisdom, understanding, and knowledge from the Word of God for the glory of God (Phil. 4:6; Prov. 24:3-4; 1 Cor. 10:31).

REFLECTION

The home is not only for private living, but a base of dominion and culture-making. Do we treat our household as a training ground for God's kingdom, or only as a shelter for ourselves?

Help for Parents: Read *Proverbs 24:3–4*. As a family, list three areas where prayer, wisdom, understanding, and knowledge should guide your home (finances, hospitality, learning, worship, etc.). Pray for God's wisdom to order each.

Inheritance: Spiritual and Material

46 **Q.** What long-term investment does God direct parents to undertake?

A: To wisely leave an inheritance to their children and grandchildren (Prov. 13:22; 2 Cor. 12:14).

47 **Q.** What should this inheritance consist of?

A. At least two things:

- A spiritual inheritance, marked by a rich heritage in the ways and works of God (Gen. 18:19; Deut. 4:8-9; 6:4-7; 32:46-47; Ps. 78:1-7; 145:4; 2 Tim. 1:5; 3:14-15);
- A physical inheritance, marked by houses, property, and other forms of material wealth (Prov. 19:14; Num. 27:6-11; Deut. 21:15-17).

48 **Q.** Which inheritance is more important to leave to children?

A. A spiritual inheritance, which is incorruptible, and does not rust or fade (3 John 1:4; Matt. 6:19-21; 1 Pet. 1:3-5; Acts 20:32-35; Col. 3:23-24).

REFLECTION

Scripture calls parents to leave their children both a spiritual inheritance in Christ and, if possible, a physical inheritance. Which of these is our family currently emphasizing more? Which needs growth?

Help for Parents: Share a testimony of how God has worked in your life or in a past generation. Then ask your children: "What do you want to remember about God when you are grown?" Write their answers in a journal as a family record of faith.

Caring for Parents and Extended Family

49 **Q.** Who does God ordain to be the primary caretaker of the extended family members?

A. The family—first and foremost—is called to take care of its own, rather than look to the church or state for earthly provision (1 Tim. 5:8).

50 **Q.** What are the family's obligations to aging parents?

A. There are at least three:

- To honor them perpetually (Exod. 20:12; Eph. 6:2-3);
- To care for their needs, particularly when they cannot adequately care for themselves (John 19:25-27; 1 Tim. 5:8);
- To strive to ensure their personal safety and welfare, especially in hard times (1 Sam. 22:3-4).

51 **Q.** What are a family's obligations to widows and orphans?

A. To care for their needs, particularly when they cannot adequately care for themselves (James 1:27; Isa. 1:17; 1 Tim. 5:4, 8).

REFLECTION

God places responsibility for care of aging parents, widows, and orphans first upon the family. Do we see caring for family members not as a burden, but as obedience to God?

Help for Parents: Read *1 Timothy 5:8*. As a family, discuss one way you can honor grandparents or an older family member this month. Make a plan (a visit, a letter, or practical help).

The Church as Safety Net

52 **Q.** What other institution should help the family with physical provision, whenever the extended family cannot do so?

A. The church, not the state, should serve as a safety net for the family, exercising care for a family's needs with wise discretion and clear accountability (1 Tim. 5:3-8; James 1:27; Gal. 2:10; Prov. 22:9; 31:20).

REFLECTION

When families cannot provide, God appoints the church—not the state—as the safety net. Does our family look to the right place for help, and do we contribute to the care of others in need?

Help for Parents: Read *James 1:27*. As a family, identify one widow, orphan, or family in need your church is aware of. Pray for them by name, and consider one tangible act of service.

The Family and the Nation

53 **Q.** How does the state of the family impact the state of the nation?

A. In at least two ways:

- When the family flourishes, the nation is strong (Deut. 32:46-47);
- When the family flounders, the nation becomes weak and is judged (Judg. 2:10-15).

54 **Q.** When God's people find themselves in a land under judgment, how should they respond?

A. To build, dwell, and plant, and pursue godly marriage and offspring (Jer. 29:4-7; Mal. 2:15).

REFLECTION

The strength of a nation rests on the strength of its families. When families crumble, nations fall under judgment. Are we preparing our household to be a strong witness even in a judged land?

Help for Parents: Read *Jeremiah 29:4–7*. Ask: "What would it look like for our family to 'build, plant, and dwell' faithfully even if our land faced judgment?" Pray that your family would be faithful wherever God has placed you.

Family Discussion

For Fathers to Ask at the Table

1. Why do you think God gave the family—not the church or the state—the first responsibility to care for the earth?
2. What kind of inheritance is most valuable to pass on to our children and grandchildren? Why?
3. How does our family's faithfulness at home affect the strength of our church, community, and nation?

For Children (Simpler Prompts)

1. Who did God tell to take care of the earth—people or animals?
2. What is more important: toys and money, or knowing and loving God?
3. How can we show honor to our parents and grandparents?

Try This Tonight

Read *Genesis 1:26–28* and *Proverbs 13:22* together. Ask each family member to share one way they can be a good caretaker—whether at home, in caring for others, or in using what God has given wisely. Close in prayer, thanking God for both the spiritual and physical blessings He provides.

Memory Verse

> *"But seek first the kingdom of God and His righteousness, and all these things shall be added to you."—Matthew 6:33*

Hymn

"This Is My Father's World"

Manhood

A Man's First Duty

55 **Q.** What is a man's first duty?

A. To love God with all his heart, soul, mind, and strength (Deut. 6:5; Matt. 22:37-38; Mark 12:30; Luke 10:27).

56 **Q.** How does man's love for God manifest?

A. By God's enabling grace, it compels him to believe, with true faith and humble repentance, in the name and saving work of the Lord Jesus Christ and to seek Christ's glory by living in obedience to Him (1 John 4:19; Eph. 2:8-10; Acts 4:12; 16:31; Isa. 66:2; Ps. 51:3; 1 Cor. 10:31; 1 John 2:3-6).

The Essence of Manhood

57 **Q.** What is the essence of manhood?

A. In submission to Christ, a man is to show leadership in his dominion calling, taking personal responsibility for those under his care, acting courageously and sacrificially, with love, for their good (John 14:15; Gen. 1:28; 1 Cor. 11:3, 8-9; Eph.

5:25-33; 1 Cor. 16:13-14; Josh. 1:6-7; 1 Kings 2:1-2).

58 **Q.** What directly undermines godly manhood?

A. At least three things:

- When men act in pride, mocking their head, Christ, whom they are bound to humbly serve and represent (1 Cor. 11:3; 4:7; 2 Cor. 3:5; Eph. 5:25-33);
- When men passively abdicate their leadership role and fail to take personal responsibility for those under their care (Gen. 3; 1 Sam. 3:12-13; 1 Kings 1:6; Rom. 5:12-14);
- When men act like women (Nah. 3:13; Isa. 19:16; Jer. 50:37; Judg. 4:4-9; 1 Cor. 6:9; 16:13).

REFLECTION

True Christian manhood is not about pride or dominance, but about taking responsibility, leading with courage, and sacrificing for the good of others. How does our home reflect these qualities of Christlike manhood?

Help for Parents: Read *1 Corinthians 16:13–14*. Ask sons: "What does it mean to act like a man in God's eyes?" Ask daughters: "What do you hope to see in godly men?" Pray for the men and boys in your home to grow into this calling.

Responsibility and Accountability

59 **Q.** When men act in pride in their leadership role, what often follows?

A. God brings destruction (Prov. 15:25; 16:18; 29:23; 2 Sam. 22:28; 1 Pet. 5:5-7).

60 **Q.** When Adam and Eve sinned, who did God hold chiefly responsible?

A. Adam (Rom. 5:12-14).

61 **Q.** What principle do we learn from this fact as it pertains to the family?

A. That God holds husbands and fathers covenantally responsible for how they lead their families (Gen. 18:19; 35:1-4; Ps. 128; 1 Sam. 3:12-14).

REFLECTION

God held Adam accountable for his family's sin, showing that fathers bear a covenantal responsibility. Are we as men embracing responsibility, or are we tempted to excuse or avoid it?

Help for Parents: Read *Genesis 18:19*. Share with your children one way you feel the weight of responsibility for your family, then ask them to pray for you in that area.

Blessing or Judgment

62 **Q.** What is the result when men faithfully discharge their leadership role in the family?

A. As a general rule, God blesses their family, according to His wisdom, often for generations (Deut. 7:9; Ps. 103:17-18; 128:1-6).

63 **Q.** What is the result when men abdicate their leadership role in the family?

A. Chaos and God's judgment, which often carries on for generations (Exod. 34:7; 1 Sam. 3:11-14).

REFLECTION

When men lead faithfully, according to God's Word, their families are generally blessed; when they abdicate, sin, chaos, and God's judgment often follow for generations. How does our family show trust in God's pattern of blessing through faithfulness?

Help for Parents: Read *Psalm 128*. As a family, talk about what blessings God has already given. Then pray for His continued mercy on your family line.

Spiritual and Physical Protection

64 **Q.** What is a man's role whenever his family is threatened with spiritual harm?

A. To decisively meet the threat and take whatever steps are necessary to neutralize its impact (Gen. 35:1-4; Josh. 24:14-15; Ps. 144:11-15; Eph. 5:25; 1 Pet. 3:7).

65 **Q.** What is a man's role whenever women and children are threatened with physical harm?

A. To seek their physical protection, even giving his life if necessary (Eph. 5:25; 1 Pet. 3:7; 1 Sam. 30:1-19).

66 **Q.** Why is the protection of the family chiefly the man's role and not the woman's?

A. Because God designed men, not women, to be the primary protectors of their families, neighbors, and nations (Gen. 32:11; 33:1-3; Deut. 22:5; Josh. 1:14-15; 1 Sam. 30:1-19; Eph. 5:25-28).

67 **Q.** Is the woman's role to protect and exercise authority erased by the man?

A. No. It is also the woman's responsibility to exercise protection and authority under the authority of her husband (Hos. 13:8; Luke 2:7; Prov. 1:8; 31:10-31).

REFLECTION

A man's role is to shield his family—spiritually by resisting sin and false teaching, and physically by protecting from harm. Are the men of our home alert and ready to defend both body and soul?

Help for Parents: Read *Joshua 24:14–15*. Lead the family in declaring together: *"As for me and my house, we will serve the LORD."* Choose one concrete step this week to guard your home (e.g., limiting harmful influences, setting aside prayer for spiritual protection).

Manhood in War and Defense

68 **Q.** Whenever war is necessary, who in the family is to take up combat roles in war?

A. God calls men, not women, to take up combat roles in war (Josh. 1:14-15; 6:3; Num. 1:2-3; Deut. 22:5).

69 **Q.** How should Christians view the advocacy of women in combat?

A. As a shameful perversion of God's moral order (Josh. 1:14-15; 6:3; Num. 1:2-3).

REFLECTION

Scripture calls men, not women, to take up combat roles in defense of family and nation. When men neglect their duty, society suffers. Do we as a family respect God's order in how protection is assigned?

Help for Parents: Read *Deuteronomy 22:5* and discuss the importance of men and women each fulfilling their God-given roles. With sons, talk about courage and self-sacrifice. With daughters, talk about the blessing of being protected and cared for.

Training Boys into Men

70 **Q.** How should boys be trained?

A. To become strong leaders, equipped to provide for others and to protect those who are weaker than themselves (1 Cor. 16:13-14; Josh. 1:6-7; 1 Kings 2:1-2; 1 Cor. 11:3; Eph. 5:25-33; 1 Pet. 3:7).

REFLECTION

Boys are not born ready for manhood—they must be trained to lead, provide, and protect to prepare them to be the head of their home. How are we actively shaping our sons (and encouraging our daughters to honor biblical manhood and headship)?

Help for Parents: Read *1 Kings 2:1–2*. Encourage your sons with one area where you see growth toward manhood. Invite them to ask questions about manhood. Pray that God would raise up strong, godly men from your family.

Family Discussion

For Fathers to Ask at the Table

1. Why does God hold men especially responsible for their families?
2. What happens when men faithfully lead with love and courage? What happens when they fail?
3. How can our family encourage boys to grow into godly men?

For Children (Simpler Prompts)

1. What should a good man do for his family?
2. Who did God hold responsible when Adam and Eve sinned?
3. How should boys show courage toward girls?

Try This Tonight

Read *1 Corinthians 16:13–14* (ESV) aloud: *"Be watchful, stand firm in the faith, act like men, be strong. Let all that you do be done in love."*

Ask each family member to share one practical way they can uphold men and boys. Close in prayer, asking God to raise up strong and loving men in your family.

Memory Verse

> *"Be watchful, stand firm in the faith, act like men, be strong. Let all that you do be done in love."—1 Corinthians 16:13–14 (ESV)*

Hymn

"Rise Up, O Men of God"

Womanhood

A Woman's First Duty

71 **Q.** What is a woman's first duty?

A. To love God with all her heart, soul, mind, and strength (Deut. 6:5; Matt. 22:37-38; Mark 12:30; Luke 10:27).

72 **Q.** How does a woman's love for God manifest?

A. By God's enabling grace, it compels her to believe, with true faith and humble repentance, in the name and saving work of the Lord Jesus Christ and to seek Christ's glory by living in obedience to Him (1 John 4:19; Eph. 2:8-10; Acts 4:12; 16:31; Isa. 66:2; Ps. 51:3; 1 Cor. 10:31; 1 John 2:3-6).

The Essence of Womanhood

73 **Q.** What is the essence of womanhood in marriage?

A. Adorned with respectful submission to Christ, she is to help her husband fulfill his dominion calling, playing a supportive role as a wise counselor, nurturer, domestic entrepreneur, and faithful homekeeper, with a gentle and quiet spirit, with all respect (John 14:15; Gen. 1:28; 2:18, 21-24; 1 Cor. 11:3, 8-9; Eph. 5:22-24; Prov. 8:1-11; 14:1; Isa. 49:15; 66:12-13; Rom. 16:1-2; 1 Thess. 2:7; Prov. 31:10-31; Titus 2:3-5; 1 Pet. 3:1-6).

74 **Q.** What is the value of a virtuous woman?

A. Her worth is far above rubies (Prov. 31:10).

REFLECTION

God calls wives to support their husbands with wisdom, respect, and a gentle spirit. Scripture describes a virtuous woman as worth far more than rubies. Do we recognize womanhood as a crown of God's creation, reflecting His goodness?

Help for Parents: Read *Proverbs 31:10–12*. Ask: "What are some ways women in our family bring blessing to others?" Encourage daughters to see the high worth of biblical womanhood, and sons to value it rightly.

Dangers That Undermine Womanhood

75 **Q.** What directly undermines virtuous womanhood?

A. At least three things:

- When women act in pride, spurning their earthly

head (thus mocking God), whom they are bound to submissively serve and represent (1 Cor. 11:3, 8-9; Prov. 30:21-23; Isa. 3:12, 16-4:1; 4:7; Eph. 5:21-24, 33);

- When women tear down rather than build up their households, as well as the households of others, through foolish, contentious, and self-centered behavior (Prov. 14:1; 9:13-18; 21:9; 25:24; 1 Tim. 5:11-14);
- When women seek to attract, seduce, manipulate, or dominate men through sinful desire or sexual allurement such as Delilah, Jezebel, the ungodly women in Proverbs, Herodius, and the metaphorical harlot of Babylon (Judg. 16; 1 Kings 16:31-33; 18:1-21:26; 2 Kings 9:30-37; Prov. 2:16-19; 5:3-14; 6:24-29; 7:1-27; Mark 6:17-28; Rev. 2:20; 17:3-6).

76 **Q.** When women act in pride, what often follows?

A. God brings them to open shame (Isa. 3:16-4:1; 2 Kings 9:30-37).

REFLECTION

Pride, foolishness, and seductive manipulation all tear down homes and mock God's order. These temptations are real in every generation. Are we alert to ways our culture encourages women to reject God's design?

Help for Parents: Read *Proverbs 14:1.* With daughters, ask: "What builds up a home?" With sons, ask: "How can you encourage women in your life to walk in God's ways?" Pray for discernment and purity in your household.

The Unique Blessing of Motherhood

77 **Q.** What blessing did God uniquely grant to women?

A. To be the bearers of children (Gen. 3:15, 20, 4:1; 21:1-2; 24:60; 29:30-35; 30:17-24; 1 Sam. 2:21; Ps. 113:5-9; 128:3; Luke 1:24-25; Heb. 11:11; 1 Tim. 2:15).

78 **Q.** After the Fall, what did God promise Eve would come through the woman as childbearer?

A. That the Messiah would come through her seed, who would bring salvation to mankind and crush the head of Satan (Gen. 3:15; Matt. 1:18-23; Luke 1:26-55).

REFLECTION

God granted women the extraordinary privilege of bearing children, through whom He promised the Messiah. Motherhood is not a burden but a blessing tied to God's salvation plan. How does our family honor and support this gift?

Help for Parents: Read *Genesis 3:15* and *Luke 1:46–48*. Talk about how Jesus came into the world through a woman, fulfilling God's promise. Then thank God for the mothers and grandmothers He has placed in your family.

The Teaching Role of Women

79 **Q.** What teaching roles does God call women to undertake?

A. Three:

- To impart wisdom to their children and grandchildren (Prov. 1:8-9; 31:1, 26; 2 Tim. 1:5; 3:15);
- To explain the Gospel to children under their care and catechize them when the husband is gone (Prov. 1:8-9; 31:1, 26; 2 Tim. 1:5; 3:15);
- To teach godly womanhood to younger women (Titus 2:3-5).

REFLECTION

God calls women to teach children and younger women in godliness. Their influence spans generations. How do we see this legacy at work in our own family?

Help for Parents: Read *2 Timothy 1:5*. Invite children to share something they've learned from their mother or grandmother about following Jesus.

True Beauty

80 **Q.** How are women to steward their God-given beauty?

A. Rather than flaunting their outer beauty through lavish adornments, they are to dress modestly, showing forth their inner beauty with a gentle and quiet spirit (Isa. 3:16-26; 1 Tim. 2:9-10; 1 Pet. 3:3-4).

81 **Q.** What does it mean that the woman is the weaker vessel?

A. This does not mean that she is weaker spiritually and intellectually, but that she is, generally by nature, weaker physically and emotionally, compared to men (Prov. 31:10-31; Heb. 11:11; Isa. 19:16; Jer. 51:30; Nah. 3:12-13).

82 **Q.** Although women are called the "weaker vessel" compared to men, can they still be strong in the Lord?

A. Through faith and by God's grace, virtuous women are to be girded with strength to accomplish great things (1 Pet. 3:7; Prov. 31:17, 25; Eph. 6:10; Prov. 31:10-31; Heb. 11:11).

REFLECTION

The world prizes outward charm and adornment, but God delights in the inner beauty of a gentle and quiet spirit. Do we pursue beauty God values, or beauty the world rewards?

Help for Parents: Read *1 Peter 3:3–4*. With daughters, discuss what "true beauty" means. With sons, ask: "What kind of beauty should you prize most in a future wife?" Pray for purity of heart and humility.

Training Girls to be Women

83 **Q.** How should girls be trained?

A. To fulfill their creation order role as virtuous women, prepared to help husbands pursue their dominion callings in the Lord, bringing glory to God in all their efforts (Eph. 6:10; Prov. 31:10-31; Gen. 1:28; 2:18, 21-24; 1 Cor. 11:3, 8-9; 10:31).

REFLECTION

Girls must be trained to embrace their creation order calling—to grow into women who strengthen homes, marriages, and the church. How are we preparing the next generation to rejoice in this calling?

Help for Parents: Read *Titus 2:3–5*. Encourage daughters by highlighting strengths you see in them that reflect biblical womanhood. Ask sons how they can honor and protect their sisters.

Family Discussion

For Fathers to Ask at the Table

1. Why does the Bible say the worth of a virtuous woman is "far above rubies"?
2. How does a woman's supportive role in marriage show the beauty of God's design?
3. What does it mean for women to display true beauty with a "gentle and quiet spirit"?

For Children (Simpler Prompts)

1. Who made girls and gave them their special role?
2. What makes a woman truly beautiful in God's

eyes?

3. How can we thank God for mothers, grandmothers, and sisters?

Try This Tonight

Read *Proverbs 31:10–31* together. Ask each child to share one way they see God's goodness in their mother (or another godly woman they know). Close in prayer, thanking God for the gift of virtuous women and asking Him to help the girls in your family grow strong in the Lord.

Memory Verse

> *"Charm is deceitful and beauty is passing, but a woman who fears the LORD, she shall be praised."—Proverbs 31:30*

Hymn

"Take My Life, and Let It Be"

Preparing for and Pursuing Marriage

Marriage as God's Norm

84 **Q.** Should most people expect to get married?

A. Because marriage is an integral part of God's created order, most people should expect to get married and thus should prepare for it (Gen. 1:26-28; 2:18, 21-24).

REFLECTION

Most people should expect marriage because it is part of God's created order. To prepare well is to honor Him. Do we view marriage as a holy calling, not merely a personal choice?

Help for Parents: Read *Genesis 2:18*. Ask your children: "Why do you think God said it was not good for man to be alone?" Pray for each child's future, whether marriage or singleness, that they would glorify God in their calling.

Preparing for Marriage

85 **Q.** How should a man prepare for marriage?

A. By striving to become like Jesus Christ and seeking first His kingdom, he is to become a strong and courageous man, equipped to provide for his future wife and family, both spiritually and physically, and to protect them from harm (Phil. 2:5-8; Matt. 6:33; 1 Cor. 16:13-14; Josh. 1:6-7; 1 Kings 2:1-2; 1 Cor. 11:3; 1 Tim. 5:8; Eph. 5:25-33; Isa. 38:19; 1 Pet. 3:7; Gen. 32:11; 33:1-3; 35:1-4; Josh. 24:14-15; Ps. 144:11-15).

86 **Q.** How should a woman prepare for marriage?

A. By striving to become like Jesus Christ and seeking first His kingdom, she is to become a strong and virtuous woman, prepared to aid her future husband fulfill His dominion calling and to look well to the way of his household (Phil. 2:5-8; Matt. 6:33; Eph. 6:10; Prov. 31:10; Gen. 1:28; 2:18, 21-24; 1 Cor. 11:3, 8-9; Prov. 14:1; 31:10-31; Titus 2:3-5).

REFLECTION

Men are to prepare by learning to lead, protect, and provide; women by learning to support, nurture, and build. Both are called to become more like

Christ. How are we training our hearts for future faithfulness?

Help for Parents: Read *Ephesians 5:25–27* for sons and *Proverbs 31:10–12* for daughters. Ask: "What is one way you can grow right now to prepare for being a godly husband or wife?"

When to Marry and When Not to

87 **Q.** When should Christians pursue marriage?

A. Whenever they can marry in the Lord and be equally yoked (Gen. 2:18; Amos 3:3; 2 Cor. 6:14-16; 1 Cor. 7:39; Deut. 7:3-4; Josh. 23:11-13).

88 **Q.** When should Christians not pursue marriage?

A. In three instances:

- Whenever they cannot marry in the Lord and be equally yoked (Gen. 2:18; Amos 3:3; 2 Cor. 6:14-16; 1 Cor. 7:39; Deut. 7:3-4; Josh. 23:11-13);
- Whenever their parents, through wise counsel, forbid it (Prov. 1:8; 6:20-24; Exod. 20:12; Gen. 28:1-2; Judg. 14:1-3);
- Whenever they prefer a life of celibacy in good conscience (Matt. 19:12; 1 Cor. 7:7-9);
- Whenever the man does not have visible means

of supporting a family (Prov. 24:27; 1 Tim. 5:8).

REFLECTION

Christians are to marry only in the Lord, with wise counsel and readiness to provide. To ignore this is to invite hardship. Do we submit our desires to God's timing and His boundaries?

Help for Parents: Read *2 Corinthians 6:14*. Talk about what it means to be "equally yoked." Encourage your children to trust that God's commands are for their good and protection.

Contentment in Singleness

89 **Q.** If one desires marriage, but is still single, how should they respond?

A. They should be content with God's perfect plan and joyfully serve Him, making the most of their single years as good stewards (Prov. 16:9; Ruth 3:12-13; Phil. 4:4, 6, 11-13; 1 Cor. 7:32-35; 15:58; Matt. 25:14-30).

90 **Q.** How can a Christian single serve the Lord?

A. As image-bearers of God and coheirs with Christ, believing singles can serve the Lord with unique focus and dedication (Gen. 1:27; Rom. 8:16-17; 1

Cor. 7:32-35; 15:58).

REFLECTION

For those waiting or given the gift of singleness, God calls for joy and fruitful service. Singleness is not wasted time—it is God's gift for a season or for life. Do we trust His wisdom for our path?

Help for Parents: Read *Proverbs 16:9*. Share a time when God directed your life differently than you expected—and how His way proved better. Ask each family member: "What helps you trust God's timing?" Close with prayer for contentment and faith.

Family Discussion

For Fathers to Ask at the Table

1. Why should most people expect to get married, and how does that shape the way we prepare for life?
2. How should men and women each prepare differently for marriage?
3. What does it mean to be "equally yoked" in marriage, and why is that important?

For Children (Simpler Prompts)

1. Who thought of marriage first—God or people?
2. What does it mean to marry "in the Lord"?
3. How can we trust God while we are waiting for His plans for us?

Try This Tonight

Read *2 Corinthians 6:14–16* and *Proverbs 24:27* together. Discuss why it matters who we marry and how God blesses preparation. Then have each family member share one way they can serve God faithfully—whether married or single. Close by praying for God's wisdom and timing in each child's life.

Memory Verse

> *"A man's heart plans his way, but the LORD directs his steps."—Proverbs 16:9*

Hymn Suggestion

"Trust and Obey"

The Duties of a Husband

Putting on the Mind of Christ

91 **Q.** How should a man prepare himself to be a husband?

A. By putting on the mind of Christ and learning to walk as He walked (Phil. 2:5-8; 1 John 2:6).

92 **Q.** What are a husband's duties toward his wife?

A. To love, lead, provide, honor, and protect her (Eph. 5:25-27; Col. 3:19; 1 Pet. 3:7).

93 **Q.** How is the husband commanded to love his wife?

A. As Christ loved the church (Eph. 5:25-27).

REFLECTION

A husband's first duty is to love his wife as Christ loved the church—selflessly, sacrificially, and faithfully. This requires humility and a Christ-centered mind. Do we see marriage as a stage for showing Christ's love?

Help for Parents: Read *Philippians 2:5–8*. Ask: "How did Jesus show humility?" Then discuss: "How should husbands follow His example in marriage?"

Christ's Example of Love

94 **Q.** How did Christ love the church?

A. He gave His very life for her (Eph. 5:25-26; Rom. 5:6-8).

95 **Q.** How must a husband be like Christ in his love for his wife?

A. In two ways:

- He is to nourish and cherish her (Eph. 5:28-30);
- He is to sanctify and cleanse her (Eph. 5:26-27).

96 **Q.** How does a husband sanctify and cleanse His wife?

A. By the washing of water by the Word (Eph. 5:26-27).

97 **Q.** How else did Christ give Himself for His bride, the church?

A. In many powerful ways:

- He leads her as a good Shepherd (John 10:11-15);
- He is always present with her (Deut. 31:6, 8; Josh. 1:5; Ps. 118:6; Heb. 13:5-6);
- He comforts her (John 14:1-3);

- He draws her with lovingkindness (Jer. 31:3);
- He prays for her (John 17:9; Heb. 7:23-25);
- He illumines her way (John 8:12);
- He nourishes her with living bread (John 6:51);
- He refreshes her with living water (John 4:14; 7:37; Rev. 21:6);
- He came to seek her (Luke 19:10);
- He came to serve her (Matt. 20:28);
- He came that she might have life more abundantly (John 10:10);
- He made her His workmanship (Eph. 2:10);
- He clothes her in white (Rev. 3:5,18);
- He keeps her as the apple of His eye (Deut. 32:10);
- He loves her as his own body (Eph. 5:28-29);
- He finds joy in sacrificing for her (Heb. 12:2; Zeph. 3:17).

REFLECTION

Christ nourishes, cherishes, sanctifies, and prays for His bride. This is the model for husbands. How does this challenge the selfishness that so often creeps into family life?

Help for Parents: Read *Ephesians 5:25–27*. Ask your children: “What are some ways you’ve seen love in action in our home?" Then pray that God would help your family reflect Christ's love more fully.

Human Limits, Divine Model

98 **Q.** Can a husband love like Christ in every respect?

A. No. Because he is not the Lord Jesus Christ, the husband cannot fully love like Him, yet by the grace, mercy, and love of God, faith in Christ, and the power of the Spirit and Word, the husband should purpose to follow Christ's example in every way he can, as His representative (Num. 23:19; Ps. 50:21; Isa. 40:18-25; Eph. 5:1, 25-32; Phil. 2:5-8).

REFLECTION

A husband can never love exactly as Christ does, yet he is called to imitate Him in every way possible. Do we strive after Christ's model even when we fall short?

Help for Parents: Read *Ephesians 5:1*. Talk briefly about what it means to be an "imitator of God." Share one area where you want to grow as a husband and father. Ask your family to pray for you.

Practical Duties of a Husband

99 **Q.** What other duties does a husband have to his wife?

A. At least six:

- To provide for her (1 Tim. 5:8);
- To honor her (1 Pet. 3:7);
- To be attentive to her eternal soul and feminine body as the weaker vessel (1 Pet. 3:7);
- To co-labor with her in taking dominion (Gen. 1:26-28; 2:15; 9:1-2; Ps. 8:6-8; James 3:7; 1 Pet. 3:7);
- To partner with her in the Gospel as a fellow heir of the grace of life (1 Pet. 3:7);
- To relinquish control over his body to her in the marriage bed (1 Cor. 7:3-5).

REFLECTION

Husbands are called to provide, honor, protect, co-labor, and partner with their wives in the Gospel. Each of these is a weighty calling. Which of these have you seen lived out in our family?

Help for Parents: Read *1 Peter 3:7*. As a family, list the six duties of a husband. Circle the one you think your family most needs to focus on this week.

Faithfulness and Purity

100 **Q.** What should be the relationship of a husband to other women?

A. He should not covet another man's wife or any other woman who is not his wife (Exod. 20:17; Prov. 5:18-20).

101 **Q.** Should a wife or a husband deny sexual relations to one another?

A. No. Their bodies belong to each other (1 Cor. 7:3-5).

REFLECTION

Husbands must be faithful in thought and deed, guarding the marriage bed and loving only their wives. How does faithfulness in marriage picture Christ's loyalty to His people?

Help for Parents: Read *Proverbs 5:18–19*. In age-appropriate ways, talk about the beauty of marital faithfulness and the danger of unfaithfulness. Pray for purity of heart and mind for everyone in the family.

Equality of Worth, Serious Consequences

102 **Q.** Is the husband more important than the wife?

A. No. They are coheirs of the gift of marriage and coheirs of Christ (1 Pet. 3:7; Gal. 3:28-29; 1 Cor. 11:11-12).

103 **Q.** What are the consequences for a husband who does not honor his wife?

A. His prayers will be hindered (1 Pet. 3:7).

REFLECTION

Husbands are not more important than wives—they are coheirs of life and grace. When husbands fail to honor their wives, even their prayers are hindered. How does this warning show God's seriousness on how a man treats his wife?

Help for Parents: Read *1 Peter 3:7*. Ask: "Why do you think God cares so much about how husbands treat their wives?" End with prayer that your home would be marked by honor, love, and unity.

Family Discussion

For Fathers to Ask at the Table

1. How is a husband's love for his wife supposed to reflect Christ's love for the church?
2. What does it mean for a husband to "nourish and cherish" his wife?
3. Why does God say a husband's prayers will be hindered if he does not honor his wife?

For Children (Simpler Prompts)

1. Who is supposed to love and protect the wife?
2. How did Jesus show His love for the church?
3. How can a husband show love to his wife every day?

Try This Tonight

Read *Ephesians 5:25–30* aloud. Ask: "What are some ways Jesus loves His church?" Then discuss: "How can husbands and fathers in our family show that kind of love at home?" Close by praying for God's help for husbands to love their wives with Christ-like devotion.

Memory Verse

> *"Husbands, love your wives, just as Christ also loved the church and gave Himself for her."—Ephesians 5:25*

Hymn

"The Church's One Foundation"

The Duties of a Wife

The Pattern of the Church

104 **Q.** What is the central illustration or pattern of the wife's role?

A. She is to become like a faithful church (Eph. 5:22-27).

105 **Q.** How does a wife fulfill her role in marriage?

A. She should learn what a glorious church looks like, and how a glorious church responds to her husband (Eph. 5:22-27; Prov. 12:4).

106 **Q.** How is a faithful church described?

A. A faithful church can be described in many ways:

- As an obedient church (Matt. 28:19-20);
- As a dependent church (John 15:1-5);
- As an adoring church (Rev. 5:9-14; 7:9-12);
- As a careful church (Deut. 4-5);
- As a church that walks in the likeness of Christ (Col. 2:6; Eph. 5:1-2; 1 John 2:6);
- As full of the Spirit (Eph. 5:18);

- As holy (Eph. 5:27);
- As a crown upon his head (Prov. 12:4).

REFLECTION

A wife is called to be like a faithful church—obedient, dependent, adoring, careful, Spirit-filled, and holy. This is not demeaning, but dignifying: she pictures the very Bride of Christ. Do we honor this calling as glorious, not burdensome?

Help for Parents: Read *Ephesians 5:22–27*. Ask: "What makes the church beautiful in God's eyes?" Then: "How does this help us understand what God calls wives to be?"

Submission as unto the Lord

107 **Q.** How should a wife relate to her husband?

A. As she does to the Lord Jesus Christ (Eph. 5:22).

108 **Q.** To whom should the wife look for leadership?

A. To her husband as her earthly head (Eph. 5:22-24).

109 **Q.** In what areas is a wife to be subject to her husband?

A. In every biblical and lawful way (Eph. 5:24).

REFLECTION

Scripture calls wives to submit to their husbands in everything, as to the Lord. This is not blind servitude, but glad obedience to Christ by honoring His design. Do we see this as God's wise and good order?

Help for Parents: Read *Ephesians 5:22*. Ask older children: "What does it mean to submit to someone else as to the Lord?" For younger children, use the example of respectfully following instructions at home or school.

Limits to Obedience

110 **Q.** Is there ever an occasion for a wife to refuse subjection to her husband?

A. Yes. A wife may refuse subjection to her husband if he leads her into anything illegal or immoral that violates the laws of God (Acts 5:29; Eph. 5:11; Ps. 119:7-8, 145).

111 **Q.** Is the husband the only authority for a wife?

A. No. A wife also exists under other authorities (Rom. 13:1-5; Heb. 13:17).

112 **Q.** What other authorities must a wife be faithful to?

A. The lawful authority of the state as well as that of a biblically-ordered church (Rom. 13:1-5; Heb. 13:17).

REFLECTION

Wives are not to obey their husbands when they are commanded to sin. God's authority always stands above human authority. Do we practice honoring authority rightly, without making it absolute?

Help for Parents: Read *Acts 5:29*. Ask: "When should we say 'no' to human authority?" Talk briefly about respecting parents, church leaders, and government, while ultimately obeying God.

Protection in Trouble

113 **Q.** If a wife is being mistreated, what should she do?

A. She should involve the elders of the church to look into the matter, for the elders of a church are ordained by God as a protection for church members. If she is being physically abused, she should involve the civil authorities (Acts 20:28-31; 1 Pet. 5:2-3; Rom. 13:1-4; 1 Pet. 2:13-14).

114 **Q.** If a wife's husband is disobedient to the Lord, what should she do?

A. Demonstrate a gentle and quiet spirit, adorned with submission (1 Pet. 3:3-6).

115 **Q.** Does winning a husband "without a word" mean that she can never say anything to her husband about his sin?

A. No. As a helpmeet, a wife has a duty to illuminate her husband with knowledge and wisdom; as a sister in Christ, she has the duty to reprove her husband with gentleness (Prov. 14:1; Gal. 6:1).

REFLECTION

God has given the church elders and civil rulers as safeguards for wives when husbands sin or abuse authority. Faithful submission does not mean tolerating evil. How does God's order protect the vulnerable?

Help for Parents: Read *1 Peter 3:3–6*. Explain that a gentle and quiet spirit does not mean silence in the face of sin. Discuss how God provides multiple layers of authority for care and accountability.

Patience and Respect

116 **Q.** How long should a wife wait for her husband to become obedient to the Word?

A. She should not grow weary in well doing, for God controls all times and seasons for His own glory (Gal. 6:9; Dan. 2:20-22; Rom. 11:34-36).

117 **Q.** What kind of attitude should a wife be careful to cultivate toward her husband?

A. A heart of respect and honor, fulfilling the laws of love in the Bible and the "one another's" in the New Testament (Eph. 5:33; 1 Pet. 3:1-6; Deut. 6:5; Rom. 13:8-10; John 13:34-35; Gal. 5:13; Eph. 4:2, 32; Col. 3:13; Rom. 12:10; James 5:16; 1 Pet. 4:9; Heb. 10:24).

REFLECTION

Wives are called to persevere in doing good, waiting on the Lord's timing, and maintaining respect even when their husbands falter. Do we trust God's sovereignty in His timing?

Help for Parents: Read *Galatians 6:9*. Ask: "Why is it hard to wait for God to act?" Pray that your family would not grow weary in well-doing but trust His perfect plan.

Examples to Follow

118 **Q.** Who are some key wives in Scripture who serve as helpful role models?

A. There are at least four:

- The Proverbs 31 woman (Prov. 31:10-31);
- Sarah (1 Pet. 3:5-6);
- Priscilla (Acts 18:24-26; Rom. 16:3-4);
- The Church (Eph. 5:22-24, 32-33).

REFLECTION

Scripture gives us models like Sarah, Priscilla, and the Proverbs 31 woman. Each shows different strengths but the same heart of faith and submission. Who are the godly women we know today who reflect this pattern?

Help for Parents: Read *Proverbs 31:10–31*. Ask your children: "Which verse in this chapter do you think best describes mom, or another godly woman you know?" Encourage your family to honor and thank God for women of faith.

Family Discussion

For Fathers to Ask at the Table

1. How does the Bible describe a wife's role by comparing her to the church?
2. What does it mean for a wife to show respect and honor toward her husband?
3. Why is it important that wives follow the example of faithful women in Scripture?

For Children (Simpler Prompts)

1. Who is the wife supposed to follow as her head?
2. What makes a wife beautiful in God's eyes?
3. Can you name one godly woman in the Bible who is a good example?

Try This Tonight

Read *1 Peter 3:3–6* together. Ask: "What kind of beauty is most precious to God?" Then have each family member thank God for one way they see His grace at work in their mother, sister(s), or another godly woman they know. Close in prayer, asking God to give wives a gentle and quiet spirit, full of faith.

Memory Verse

> *"Wives, submit to your own husbands, as to the Lord."—Ephesians 5:22*

Hymn

"May the Mind of Christ My Savior"

The Mutual Duties of Husband and Wife

One Body, One Mission

119 **Q.** What mutual responsibilities do husbands and wives share in marriage?

A. At least five:

- To regard themselves as one body (Eph. 5:30-32);
- To be fruitful and multiply (Gen. 1:28; 9:1; Mal. 2:15; John 15:1-8);
- To take dominion over the earth (Gen. 1:26; 2:15; 19-20; Ps. 8:4-8; 115:16);
- To establish Sabbath rest for all in their household (Gen. 2:2-3; Exod. 16:22-23; 20:8-11; Isa. 58:13-14; Jer. 17:21-22);
- To instruct their children in the Gospel and in godly wisdom (Deut. 6:1-9; Prov. 1:8-9; 4:1-4; 22:6; 31:1, 26; Isa. 38:19; Eph. 6:1-4).

REFLECTION

Marriage is a partnership—husband and wife are "one flesh," called to fruitfulness, dominion, Sabbath rest, and raising children in the Lord. Do we see our marriage as teamwork under God's authority?

Help for Parents: Read *Genesis 1:28*. As a couple or family, name one way you can better work together in God's mission (for example, family prayer, hospitality, stewardship, or training children). Pray together for unity and purpose.

Marriage and Eternity

120 **Q.** Will husbands and wives still be married in heaven?

A. No. *"For in the resurrection they neither marry nor are given in marriage, but are like angels of God in heaven"* (Matt. 22:30).

REFLECTION

Earthly marriage is temporary, designed to point us toward the eternal marriage of Christ and His church. Does our family live with eternity in view, or do we treat marriage as ultimate?

Help for Parents: Read *Matthew 22:30*. Ask: "What do you think it will be like to be with Jesus forever?" Use this to highlight that marriage is a picture of something greater to come.

The Greater Joy to Come

121 **Q.** Will this be a hardship or saddening for the husband and wife?

A. No, for their relationship in the new heavens and the new earth will far exceed their earthly relationship, for they will be married to Christ, experiencing no more sin, pain, suffering, or death (1 Cor. 15:41-43, 51-54; Rev. 21:1-4).

REFLECTION

In heaven, we will know a joy deeper than the best of marriages: perfect fellowship with Christ, free from sin, pain, and death. How does this hope shape the way we love one another now?

Help for Parents: Read *Revelation 21:1–4*. Ask each family member: "What are you most looking forward to in the new heavens and new earth?" Close by thanking Jesus for the eternal marriage supper of the Lamb.

Family Discussion

For Fathers to Ask at the Table

1. What are some responsibilities that both

husbands and wives share together in marriage?

2. How do husband and wife show that they are "one body" in the Lord?
3. Why won't marriage continue in heaven, and what greater joy will believers share instead?

For Children (Simpler Prompts)

1. What are some things both Mom and Dad are supposed to do together?
2. Who do husbands and wives belong to in heaven?
3. How can children see God's goodness in the way their parents work together?

Try This Tonight

Read *Genesis 1:27–28* and *Ephesians 6:1–4*. Ask: "What does God want both husbands and wives to do for their children?" Then have each parent share one way they can work together in teaching, helping, or leading the family this week. Close in prayer, thanking God for making marriage a partnership to glorify Him.

Memory Verse

> *"So then, they are no longer two but one flesh. Therefore what God has joined together, let not man separate."—Matthew 19:6*

Hymn Suggestions

"O Give Us Homes" also known as, *"A Christian Home"*

The Blessing of Children

Fruitfulness as a Command

122 **Q.** What is the first command God gave to Adam and Eve as a couple?

A. To be fruitful and multiply (Gen. 1:28).

123 **Q.** When did God command our first parents to be fruitful and multiply?

A. To Adam and Eve at the close of creation week (Gen. 1:28, 31).

124 **Q.** What was the first command God gave to Noah and his sons after the Flood?

A. To be fruitful and multiply (Gen. 9:1, 7).

125 **Q.** In view of this command, how should married couples approach having children?

A. They should desire and prioritize the blessing of children, praying that God, in His providence, would open the womb (Gen. 1:28; 9:1, 7; 24:60; 25:21; 30:17-18; 1 Sam. 1:27-28; Isa. 66:9).

REFLECTION

The very first command God gave mankind was to "be fruitful and multiply." Children are not an afterthought—they are part of God's plan for creation, for the spread of the Gospel, and the advancement of His kingdom. Do we treasure children as central to God's design?

Help for Parents: Read *Genesis 1:28*. Ask: "Why do you think God made children part of His first command to the first family?" Invite each family member to share what blessings they see in younger siblings, cousins, or children in the church.

God's Purposes in Procreation

126 **Q.** Why is procreation central to God's plan?[4]

A. Procreation is central for at least three reasons:

- So that the earth would be inhabited (Isa. 45:18; Gen. 1:28; Gen. 9:1, 7, 19);
- So that godly offspring would come forth (Mal. 2:15; Gen. 18:17-19; Isa. 58:12);
- So that God's eternal plan for salvation would be accomplished (Gen. 3:15; Matt. 1:18-23; Luke 1:26-55).

4. **procreation** – the physical act of union between man and woman that brings forth children, whenever God opens the womb.

REFLECTION

Children fill the earth, raise up godly generations, and carry forward God's salvation plan. Every new life is a testimony that God is still at work. How do we see His plan in our family story?

Help for Parents: Read *Malachi 2:15*. Ask: "What does it mean that God seeks 'godly offspring'?" Pray for your children—by name—that they would grow as arrows for Christ's kingdom.

The God Who Opens and Closes the Womb

127 **Q.** Who opens and closes the womb?

A. God (Gen. 20:17-18; 21:1-2; 25:21; 29:30-31; 30:1-2, 17-22; Exod. 23:25-26; Lev. 26:9; Deut. 1:10; Ruth 4:13; 1 Sam. 1:5-6, 17-20; 2:21; Isa. 66:9).

128 **Q.** How does God's Word describe children?

A. God describes children in at least four ways:

- As a blessing (Gen. 17:15-17; 26:4-5; 28:1-3; Lev. 26:3, 9; Deut. 6:1-3; 7:12-14; 28:4, 11; Job 42:12-15; Ps. 107:38, 41; 128:1-6; Isa. 51:2);
- As a gift (Gen. 4:1; 33:4-5; 48:9; Ruth 4:12-13; 1 Sam. 2:21; 1 Chron. 25:4-5; 28:5; Ps. 113:8-9;

Isa. 8:18);

- As a reward (Ps. 127:3);
- As a heritage (Ps. 127:3).

129 **Q.** How is a barren womb described in Scripture?

A. In at least three ways:

- As a curse (Lev. 26:21-22; Deut. 28:15, 18, 62-63; Hos. 9:11);
- As a reproach (Gen. 30:22-23; Luke 1:24-25);
- As under the providence of God who opens and closes the womb (1 Sam. 1:6; Gen. 11:30; 20:18; 21:1-2; Ps. 139:13-16; Isa. 66:9-13; Jer. 1:5).

REFLECTION

Children are always described as blessings, gifts, rewards, and heritage. Yet God alone opens and closes the womb. Do we trust Him in both abundance and barrenness?

Help for Parents: Read *Psalm 127:3*. Ask: "What does it mean to call children a 'heritage from the LORD'?" With sensitivity, talk about trusting God's timing, even when it is hard.

Barrenness and God's Purposes

130 **Q.** Besides judgment, what is another reason God often ordains seasons of barrenness?

A. To test and build our faith and to prove God's wise yet hidden purposes (Gen. 18:9-14; 21:1-3; 25:21; Heb. 11:11; 1 Sam. 1:1-2:11; Luke 1:13-14, 36-37).

131 **Q.** When God withholds childbearing, how should one respond?

A. Trust God's plan and acknowledge that His ways are perfect (Isa. 46:9-10; Prov. 3:5-6; 1 Sam 2:2-4; Heb. 11:6, 11; 1 Chron. 16:11; Deut. 32:4; Isa. 55:8-9; Prov. 19:21).

REFLECTION

Seasons of barrenness test faith, yet God often uses them to display His power and wisdom. Many of Scripture's greatest children (Isaac, Samuel, John the Baptist) were born after long waiting. Do we see waiting as wasted—or as God's preparation?

Help for Parents: Read *1 Samuel 1:27–28*. Share Hannah's testimony. Ask: "How does waiting sometimes make God's blessing even more precious?" Pray for faith in God's hidden purposes.

Adoption as God's Model

132 **Q.** What alternative to natural childbearing does God personally model in Scripture for having children?

A. Adoption (Eph. 1:5; Gal. 4:4-7; Ps. 27:10; John 14:18; 1 John 3:1).

REFLECTION

God Himself adopts His children through Christ. Adoption is not second-best, but a glorious reflection of the Gospel. How might our family support adoption or care for the fatherless?

Help for Parents: Read *Ephesians 1:5*. Ask: "What does it mean that God adopted us into His family?" Discuss ways you can show hospitality or care for children who need family love.

Children in Troubled Times

133 **Q.** During difficult and threatening times, how should God's people approach procreation?

A. To continue seeking the blessing of children, trusting God to sustain them (Exod. 1:12-21; Jer. 29:4-5).

134 **Q.** What examples are there in Scripture that encourage us to pursue bearing children in troubled

times?

A. Two:

- The Hebrew slaves in Egypt (Exod. 1:12-21);
- The Israelite captives in Babylon (Jer. 29:4-5).

REFLECTION

Even in slavery in Egypt or exile in Babylon, God's people bore children, trusting His promise. To raise children in hard times is an act of faith that God sustains His people. Do we trust God's care enough to welcome children, even in uncertainty?

Help for Parents: Read *Jeremiah 29:5–7*. Ask: "Why would God tell His people to build families in exile?" Talk about how your family can live faithfully even when the world seems dark.

Family Discussion

For Fathers to Ask at the Table

1. What does God's first command to Adam and Eve—"be fruitful and multiply"—tell us about His priorities for parents having children?
2. How does the Bible describe children—as a burden or as a blessing?

3. When God gives seasons of barrenness or waiting, how should families respond in faith?

For Children (Simpler Prompts)

1. Who gives children to families?
2. What does the Bible call children: a gift or a curse?
3. How can we show God that we are thankful for the blessing of children?

Try This Tonight

Read *Psalm 127:3–5* together. Ask: "Why does God call children a reward and heritage?" Then invite each family member to share one reason they are thankful for the children (or siblings) God has given to your family. Close with prayer, thanking God for the gift of children and asking Him to help you see them as a blessing.

Memory Verse

> *"Behold, children are a heritage from the LORD, the fruit of the womb is a reward."*—Psalm 127:3

Hymn

"Children of the Heavenly Father"

Fatherhood

God the Father as Model

135 **Q.** Who is the ultimate model for earthly fatherhood?

A. Our Heavenly Father (Luke 11:11-13: Heb. 12:4-9).

136 **Q.** What qualities does God the Father show toward His children?

A. He initiates, plans, provides, protects, and leads His children in all things (Isa. 46:9-11; Rom. 8:28-30; John 3:16; 1 Cor. 8:6).

137 **Q.** What is one key way God the Father initiates, plans, and leads His children?

A. He initiates, sustains, and completes their salvation by His Word and Spirit (John 3:16; Rom. 8:28-30; Eph. 1:3-14; 2 Tim. 2:9-10; Isa. 63:16; 64:4-8; 2 Thess. 2:13-16).

REFLECTION

Earthly fathers are to look to our Heavenly Father, who initiates, provides, protects, and leads His children perfectly. Do we measure our fatherhood by the world's standards—or by God's?

Help for Parents: Read *Ephesians 1:3–5*. Share with your children: "This is how God treats us—and I want to follow His example." Ask them: "What is one way God has cared for you?"

God's Fatherly Qualities

138 **Q.** What other qualities does God the Father show toward His children?

A. There are many:

- He loves them with an everlasting love (Jer. 31:3; 1 John 3:1; Eph. 2:4-5);
- He blesses them (Eph. 1:3);
- He shows mercy to them (Luke 6:36; Eph. 2:4; Ps. 103:8, 11, 17);
- He acts kindly toward them (Eph. 2:7; Titus 3:4-7);
- He gives grace to them (Eph. 2:8-9);
- He shows compassion to them in their frailty (Ps. 103:13-14);

- He bestows good gifts to them (Matt. 7:7-11; James 1:17);
- He forgives their sins (Eph. 1:7; 4:32; Luke 11:2-4);
- He molds and shapes them (Isa. 64:8);
- He instructs them in the way they should go (Ps. 25:8-10; 32:8; Isa. 48:17; John 6:45);
- He grants them wisdom (Ps. 51:6; Prov. 2:6; Eph. 1:17);
- He leads them in truth (Ps. 25:5; 43:3);
- He teaches them to fight (2 Sam. 22:35; Ps. 144:1);
- He equips them to do His will (Heb. 13:20-21; Exod. 4:11-12);
- He rescues them out of distress (Ps. 107:28);
- He chastens them for disobedience (Heb. 12:4-9);
- He protects them from harm (Ps. 46:1; 121:5-8);
- He preserves them until the end (John 10:28).

REFLECTION

God shows love, mercy, discipline, provision, and preservation. Every act of fatherhood should mirror at least some of these qualities. Do our children see glimpses of God's character in us?

Help for Parents: Read *Psalm 103:13–14*. Ask: "How does God show compassion to His children?"

Then talk together about one practical way a father can show compassion in the home this week.

Responsibilities of Earthly Fathers

139 **Q.** Even as earthly fathers draw from God the Father's example, what specific responsibilities does Scripture require of them toward their children?

A. There are many:

- To bring them up in the training and admonition of the Lord (Eph. 6:4);
- To guide them in truth and wisdom (Isa. 38:19; Prov. 2:1-5; 5:1);
- To teach them to love God with all their heart, soul, and might (Deut. 6:4-7);
- To disciple them in God's ways through every facet of life (Deut. 6:6-7);
- To call them to strength and courage (1 Kings 2:2; 1 Chron. 28:10, 20);
- To charge them to obey God's Word in everything (Gen. 18:19; 1 Kings 2:3; 1 Chron. 28:8);
- To exhort them to keep their heart with all diligence (Prov. 4:23);
- To warn them against following evil men and women (Prov. 1:10-19; 5:1-13; 6:20-7:1-27);

- To show them the way of salvation (2 Tim. 3:15);
- To correct them when they disobey (Prov. 6:23; 27:5; Prov. 19:18; 22:15; 23:13-14);
- To be on high alert for ungodly influences that may affect them and take decisive steps to neutralize such threats (Gen. 35:2-4; Ps. 144:11-12; Prov. 13:20);
- To demonstrate godly living to them (1 Cor. 11:1; Phil. 4:9; James 3:13);
- To cry out to the Lord on their behalf (1 Chron. 29:19; Job 1:5, 2 Sam 12:16-18; Mark 9:14-29);
- To lead them in regular family devotions (Deut. 6:6-7; Ps. 78:5-7; Isa. 38:19);
- To root them in local church life with a faithful body of believers (Ps. 92:12-15; Heb. 10:24-25).

REFLECTION

Fathers must bring children up in the Lord, guiding, discipling, warning, correcting, and praying for them. Fatherhood is not passive but active, with eternal consequences. Are we alert and intentional as fathers, or are we drifting?

Help for Parents: Read *Ephesians 6:4.* Ask: "What do you think it means for a father to bring his children up in the training and admonition of the Lord?" Then pray together that fathers today would lead faithfully, and children would joyfully receive godly training.

Family Discussion

For Fathers to Ask at the Table

1. Why is God the Father the best example for earthly fathers to follow?
2. What are some of the ways God the Father cares for His children?
3. How can earthly fathers reflect God's love and leadership in the home?

For Children (Simpler Prompts)

1. Who is the best Father of all?
2. What good things does God the Father give His children?
3. How can dads show love like God the Father?

Try This Tonight

Read *Ephesians 6:4* and *Psalm 103:13–14* aloud. Ask: "How does God the Father treat His children, and how should earthly fathers treat their families?" Then have each child share one way they feel loved and cared for by their father. Close in prayer, thanking God for being the perfect Father and asking Him to help earthly fathers follow His example.

Memory Verse

> *"As a father pities his children, so the LORD pities those who fear Him."—Psalm 103:13*

Hymn

"Blest the Man that Fears Jehovah"

Motherhood

The High Calling of Motherhood

140 **Q.** What aspect of womanhood does Scripture highly exalt?

A. That of fruitful motherhood (Gen. 3:20; 24:60; 49:25; Ruth 4:11-12; Ps. 113:9; 127:3; 128:3; Ezek. 19:10-11; Luke 1:41-42, 46-48).

141 **Q.** When Adam and Eve sinned, what unique curse did God place upon women?

A. That they would experience pain in bearing children (Gen. 3:16).

142 **Q.** Despite the pain of childbearing, what is a woman's response once her child is born?

A. She rejoices over her new baby (Ps. 113:9; John 16:21).

REFLECTION

Scripture highly exalts mothers as life-bearers and nurturers, even though childbearing comes with pain since the Fall. Yet joy follows when a child is born. Do we see motherhood as God's blessing, not as a burden?

Help for Parents: Read *John 16:21*. Ask: "Why does a mother forget her pain when her baby is born?" Encourage your children to express thankfulness for their mother's love and sacrifice.

The Nurturing Heart of Mothers

143 **Q.** What instinctive quality do women possess that thrives in motherhood?

A. The quality of a compassionate nurturer (Isa. 49:15; 66:12; Luke 2:7; 1 Thess. 2:7).

144 **Q.** What is the heart cry of barren women?

A. That God would bless her with children (1 Sam. 1:10-18; Luke 1:24-25).

REFLECTION

God has given women an instinctive compassion for children, shown in Scripture and nature itself. Mothers reflect God's tender care in unique ways. How do we honor and support this gift?

Help for Parents: Read *Isaiah 49:15*. Ask your children: "What are some ways mom shows compassion every day?" Lead in a prayer thanking God for the daily kindnesses of mothers.

The Maternal Instinct across Creation

145 **Q.** Beyond women, where else in creation do we see illustrations of the maternal instinct on display?

A. In the animal kingdom (Deut. 22:6; Lam. 4:3; Hos. 13:8; Matt. 23:37).

146 **Q.** Who forms and protects children in their mother's womb?

A. God (Ps. 139:13-16).

REFLECTION

Even animals reflect something of God's design for mothers as protectors and caretakers. But human mothers show this most fully because they are made in God's image. Do we see this care as pointing us back to the Creator?

Help for Parents: Read *Psalm 139:13–16*. Talk briefly about how God forms children in the womb. Ask: "What does it mean that we are 'fearfully and wonderfully made'?"

Daily Duties of Mothers

147 **Q.** What practical day-to-day task are mothers to undertake?

A. To ensure that their children are fed, clothed, and taught the general subjects of education (Gen. 21:7; Exod. 2:7-9; 1 Sam. 1:21-23; Isa. 49:15; 66:10-13; 1 Thess. 2:7; Prov. 31:13-15, 21; Luke 2:7; Eph. 6:1-4).

148 **Q.** What spiritual day-to-day duty do mothers have toward their children?

A. To wisely teach them to follow the ways of the Lord (Deut. 6:6-9; Prov. 1:8-9; 31:1, 26; 2 Tim. 1:5; 3:15).

REFLECTION

Feeding, clothing, teaching, and training are not small tasks—they are holy work. Every meal prepared, every lesson taught, and every word of wisdom is service to Christ. Do we see ordinary motherhood as extraordinary in God's eyes?

Help for Parents: Read *2 Timothy 1:5*. Ask: "What do you think Timothy learned from his mother and grandmother?" Discuss how teaching children the Scriptures shapes lives for eternity.

Family Discussion

For Fathers to Ask at the Table

1. Why does the Bible call motherhood one of the highest blessings for women?
2. How does God use mothers to show His compassion and care?
3. What daily tasks and spiritual duties does Scripture say mothers should carry out for their children?

For Children (Simpler Prompts)

1. Who gives children to mothers?

2. What special job has God given moms to do each day?
3. How can children thank God for their mothers?

Try This Tonight

Read *2 Timothy 1:5* together. Talk about how Timothy's mother and grandmother helped him know God's Word. Then have each child share one thing they have learned about God from their mom (or another godly woman in their life). Close in prayer, thanking God for mothers who teach and nurture their children.

Memory Verse

> *"She opens her mouth with wisdom, and on her tongue is the law of kindness."—Proverbs 31:26*

Hymn

"Day by Day"

Bringing Up Children

The First Duty of Parents

149 **Q.** What is the most important duty that God gives parents as they bring up their children?

A. To love the Lord their God with all your heart, soul, and strength (Deut. 6:5).

REFLECTION

Parents cannot pass on what they do not have. Loving God with all the heart, soul, and strength must come first. Do our children see in us a living example of devotion to God?

Help for Parents: Read *Deuteronomy 6:5*. Ask: "How can we show our love for God today?" Model this love through prayer, song, and joyful obedience.

Teaching Children of Their Sin and Need of a Savior

150 **Q.** What should parents teach their children about themselves?

A. To explain their state as sinful creatures and their

need to repent and believe on the Lord Jesus Christ for salvation (Ps. 51:5; Acts 3:19; 16:31).

REFLECTION

Children are born sinners and must be lovingly taught their need for repentance and faith in Christ. If parents fail to teach this, the world, the flesh and the Devil (Eph. 2:1-3) will teach them otherwise. Do we clearly point our children to Christ daily?

Help for Parents: Read *Psalm 51:5* and *Acts 16:31*. Ask: "Why do we all need Jesus?" Lead your family in thanking God for sending His Son to save sinners.

Training and Admonition in Daily Life

151 **Q.** What other duties are required of parents toward their children?

A. There are many:

- To bring them up in the training and admonition of the Lord (Deut. 6:1-9; Prov. 4:1-4; 22:6; Isa. 38:19; Eph. 6:1-4);
- To lead them to love God with all their heart, soul, and strength, and to love their neighbor as themselves (Exod. 20:3; Matt. 22:37-39; Deut. 6:4-7; Lev. 19:18; Mark 12:30-31);

- To proclaim the great deeds of God to them (Josh. 4; Exod. 13:14; Ps. 71:18; 78:1-7; 145:4);
- To direct them to seek first Christ's kingdom and righteousness (Matt. 6:33);
- To bind and seal God's testimony in their hearts (Isa. 8:16);
- To raise them to walk in the truth (Isa. 38:19; 3 John 1:4);
- To call them to fear God and keep His commandments (Prov. 1; Eccles. 12:13; Gen. 18:19);
- To equip them to rebuild what sin has destroyed (Neh. 3-4; Isa. 58:12);
- To seek that they may be as signs and wonders in an evil day (Isa. 8:18);
- To launch them as arrows to contend with the enemies in the gates (Ps. 127:4-5; Gen. 22:17; 24:60);
- To train them to pass on the truth they have learned through earnest discipleship of others (Ps. 78:1-7; 145:4; Matt. 28:19-20; 2 Tim. 2:2);
- To pray that God's glory would shine through them in an enduring work across generations (Ps. 90:16-17; Deut. 7:9; Luke 1:49-50).

REFLECTION

Parents must saturate family life with God's Word, helping children to love Him, obey His commands, and walk in wisdom. Are we weaving God's truth into both formal teaching and casual conversations?

Help for Parents: Read *Ephesians 6:4*. Ask: "What's one way we can bring God into our daily conversations?" Try starting or ending the day with a brief Scripture reflection together.

Correction with Love

152 **Q.** How should parents respond when their children willfully disobey them?

A. They are to correct them according to the fruit of the Spirit, as God corrects His own sons (Prov. 29:15, 17; Gal. 5:22-25; Heb. 12:5-8).

153 **Q.** When children disobey, what should this correction consist of?

A. Two things:

- Verbal reproof (Prov. 6:23; 27:5; 2 Tim. 3:16-17);
- Physical correction, as necessary (Prov. 19:18; 22:15; 23:13-14).

REFLECTION

God disciplines those He loves; parents must correct their children's disobedience with love through words and, when necessary, physical discipline—never in anger, but with patience and consistency. Do our children understand discipline as love?

Help for Parents: Read *Hebrews 12:6.* Say: "We correct you because God corrects His children out of love." Ask: "How does correction help us stay on the right path?"

Building Lifelong Character

154 **Q.** What spiritual traits and practical lessons should parents teach their children?

A. There are many:

- That they might earnestly seek wisdom (Prov. 1; 3:1-18);
- That they might forsake foolish company and walk among the wise (Prov. 1:10-19; 4:14-18; 9:6; 13:20; 23:20-21; 1 Cor. 15:33);
- That they might keep their hearts from impure thoughts and the wiles of the adulteress (Job 31:1; Prov. 5:1-14; 7:1-27);
- That they might appreciate godly correction (Prov.

3:11-12; 13:18; 15:5, 31);

- That they might be diligent and industrious, not lazy (Prov. 10:4-5; 12:11; 13:4; 20:4; 21:5; 28:19);
- That they might use their tongues wisely, not foolishly (Prov. 15:2; 25:11; 29:11);
- That they might do all things with integrity (Prov. 10:9; 19:1; 20:7; 28:6; Ps. 26:1-12; 101:2-4);
- That they might seek a good name rather than riches (Prov. 22:1; Eccles. 7:1).

REFLECTION

Parents shape character by teaching diligence, purity, wisdom, integrity, and self-control. These lessons are eternal investments. Are we equipping our children to live for God, not just succeed in the world?

Help for Parents: Read *Proverbs 22:1*. Ask: "Why is having a good name (a reputation for godliness) more valuable than riches?" As a family, list qualities that make up a good reputation in God's sight.

Family Discussion

For Fathers to Ask at the Table

1. What is the most important thing parents must love and teach first as they raise their children?
2. Why must children be taught about their sin and need for Jesus?
3. How should parents respond when their children disobey, and why is this important?

For Children (Simpler Prompts)

1. Who do parents need to love most as they bring up children?
2. What does the Bible say about all people, including children, needing Jesus?
3. Why do parents correct their children?

Try This Tonight

Read *Deuteronomy 6:4–7* aloud. Talk about how God commands parents to speak of His Word "when you sit in your house, when you walk by the way, when you lie down, and when you rise up." Have each child share one way they can remember God's Word during their day. Close in prayer, asking God to help your family love Him with all your heart.

Memory Verse

> *"Train up a child in the way he should go, and when he is old he will not depart from it."—Proverbs 22:6*

Hymn

"Happy the Home When God Is There"

Duties of Sons and Daughters

The Fifth Commandment

155 **Q.** What duty does the Ten Commandments require of children?

A. Honor your father and mother (Exod. 20:12; Deut. 5:16).

156 **Q.** What promise comes when children obey the command to honor their parents?

A. It will be well with them (Exod. 20:12; Deut. 5:16; Eph. 6:2).

REFLECTION

God commands children to honor father and mother—with the promise of blessing and well-being. Obedience to parents is more than good manners; it is obedience to God. Do we treat this command as weighty?

Help for Parents: Read *Ephesians 6:2*. Ask: "What does it mean to 'honor' parents—is it only obedience, or more than that?" Pray that your children would treasure God's promise attached to this command.

True vs. False Honor

157 **Q.** What happens when children merely feign honor to their parents, while actually dishonoring them?

A. They make the command of God of no effect (Matt. 15:4-6).

REFLECTION

Pretending to honor while secretly dishonoring is hypocrisy. God looks at the heart, not just outward respect. Are we teaching our children to obey sincerely?

Help for Parents: Read *Matthew 15:4–6*. Ask: "Why does it matter to God if our hearts match our words and actions?" Encourage your children to be honest about their attitudes.

Reverence and Obedience

158 **Q.** How are children to behave in the presence of their parents?

A. With respect and reverence, honoring their

position of authority (Gen. 22:7; 27:18; Lev. 19:3).

159 **Q.** How are children to respond to their parents' commands?

A. Obey them (Eph. 6:1; Col. 3:20).

160 **Q.** In what matters must they obey them?

A. In all things biblical and lawful (Col. 3:20).

161 **Q.** Why are children to obey their parents?

A. It is right and well-pleasing to the Lord (Eph. 6:1; Col. 3:20).

REFLECTION

Children are called to respect and obey their parents in all things, for it is right and pleasing to God. This forms their training in respecting God Himself. Do our children see obedience to parents as obedience to God?

Help for Parents: Read *Colossians 3:20*. Ask: "Why does obeying parents please God?" Help your children name one way they can obey quickly and cheerfully this week.

The Blessing of Wise Commands

162 **Q.** What benefit comes from children heeding a parent's wise commands?

A. These commands will enlighten their way and keep them from personal ruin (Prov. 1:8-19; 5:1-14; 6:20-35; 7:1-27).

163 **Q.** In what other way must children follow their parents?

A. They are to follow the good example of their parents, as they wisely follow Christ (Prov. 23:26; 1 Cor. 11:1).

REFLECTION

Parents' wise instruction keeps children from ruin and points them toward Christ. Children are also called to follow their parents' godly example. Do we see obedience as protection and blessing, not a burden?

Help for Parents: Read *Proverbs 1:8–9*. Ask: "What do you think it means when it says a parent's teaching is like 'graceful ornaments'?" Talk about the beauty of listening to godly counsel.

Limits to Obedience

164 **Q.** Must children obey evil commands and follow wicked practices set forth by their parents?

A. No. In such cases, they should walk in God's ways instead (Ezek. 20:18-19; Acts 5:29).

REFLECTION

Children are not to obey when parents demand evil or disobedience to God. God's Word is always the highest authority. Do we make clear that God's commands are supreme?

Help for Parents: Read *Acts 5:29*. Ask: "What should we do if someone tells us to do something against God's Word?" Explain that obedience to God always comes first.

The Consequences of Dishonor

165 **Q.** What comes from God when children mock and dishonor their parents?

A. A curse and judgment (Deut. 27:16; Prov. 30:11-13, 17; 1 Sam. 2:23-25).

166 **Q.** How should children respond to their parents' faults?

A. While never condoning their parents' sin, they should not spitefully exploit it, but show them due respect, despite their shortcomings (Gen. 9:20-23; Deut. 27:16; Eccles. 7:20).

REFLECTION

To dishonor parents invites God's curse and judgment; to exploit and proclaim their sins in public is greater dishonor. Respect is owed even when parents are imperfect. How do we model this respect in our home?

Help for Parents: Read *Proverbs 30:17*. Ask: "Why does God take dishonor to parents so seriously?" Then talk about what it looks like to show respect even when parents sin or make mistakes.

The Joy and Grief of Parents

167 **Q.** How do parents view their children who live with wisdom?

A. As a joy and a delight (Prov. 23:24-25).

168 **Q.** How do parents view their children who live foolishly?

A. As a bitter grief to them (Prov. 17:25; Gen. 26:34-35; 1 Sam. 2:23-24).

REFLECTION

Wise children bring joy, but foolish children bring grief. Our obedience and wisdom deeply affect our parents' hearts and their reputation among brothers and sisters in Christ. Do children in our home see their choices as shaping family joy?

Help for Parents: Read *Proverbs 23:24–25*. Ask: "How can children make their parents glad?" Share one way your children's obedience or kindness has brought you joy.

Caring for Parents in Need

169 **Q.** When a parent has personal or financial needs, what should their children do?

A. Help them to the best of their ability (1 Tim. 5:3-4; Gen. 47:11-12; 1 Sam. 22:3-4).

REFLECTION

Honoring parents doesn't end in childhood. Grown children are called to provide for parents in their old age. Do we view this as a duty and privilege?

Help for Parents: Read *1 Timothy 5:4*. Ask: "How can children show love to parents and grandparents as they grow older?" Pray for a heart that delights to honor family through all stages and conditions of life.

Family Discussion

For Fathers to Ask at the Table

1. Which command in the Ten Commandments is directed to children?
2. What promise does God give to children who honor their parents?
3. How should children respond when parents sin, make mistakes, or show faults?

For Children (Simpler Prompts)

1. What does God say children must do for their father and mother?
2. What good things happen when children obey

their parents?

3. How can you show respect to your parents every day?

Try This Tonight

Read *Ephesians 6:1–3* aloud. Ask: "Why does God say it is right and pleasing for children to obey their parents?" Close in prayer, thanking God for parents, and asking Him to give your children obedient, respectful hearts.

Memory Verse

> *"Honor your father and your mother, that your days may be long upon the land which the LORD your God is giving you."—Exodus 20:12*

Hymn

"Teach Me, O Lord, Thy Holy Way"

Family Worship

What Is Family Worship?

170 **Q.** What is family worship?

A. An intentional gathering of one's family in the home (or wherever the family is, when away from home) to worship God through Scripture, song, and prayer (Ps. 118:15; Deut. 6:4-9; Josh. 1:8; Ps. 78:5-7; 119:172; 145:1-4; Isa. 8:16-18; Ps. 92:1-2; 96:2; Col. 3:16; Ps. 55:16-17; Job 1:5).

REFLECTION

Family worship is not an optional practice, but a holy, essential, daily gathering at home to pray, to read God's Word, and to sing His praises. It is a vital rhythm of gathering daily in the home. Do we treat worship at home as central to our walk with Christ?

Help for Parents: Read *Deuteronomy 6:6–7.* Ask: "Why does God tell parents to speak of His Word when we sit, walk, lie down, and rise up?" Encourage your children to see worship as a normal part of daily life.

The Daily Call

171 **Q.** How often should family worship occur?

A. Daily (Deut. 6:4-9; Josh. 1:8; Job 1:5; Ps. 55:16-17; 92:1-2; 96:2; 145:1-4).

REFLECTION

Worship is a daily essential for spiritual life in the home. Just as we daily eat and drink to strengthen the body, we daily need the Word, prayer, and song to strengthen the soul. Is our family nourished daily by God's Word?

Help for Parents: Read *Psalm 92:1–2*. Ask: "Why does this psalm say it's good to praise God morning and night?" Share one practical way your family could be more consistent in daily worship.

The Father's Responsibility

172 **Q.** Who should lead in family worship?

A. Fathers (Gen. 18:19; Josh. 24:15; Ps. 78:5-7; Isa. 38:19; Eph. 6:4).

173 **Q.** Who are fathers in Scripture that practiced family worship?

A. Noah, Abraham, Isaac, Jacob, and Job (Gen. 8:20;

12:7-8; 13:3-4; 18:19; 22:1-14; 26:23-25; 35:1-7; Job 1:5).

REFLECTION

God has entrusted fathers to lead in family worship. This is not a duty to shirk or outsource, but a privilege to embrace for the glory of Christ and the spiritual life of the family. Fathers, do you cherish this as a holy calling?

Help for Parents: Read *Joshua 24:15*. Declare: "As for me and my house, we will serve the LORD." Talk as a family about what it means to serve the Lord together.

When Fathers Are Absent

174 **Q.** When fathers are away, or are not believers, who should lead in family worship?

A. Mothers, or whoever else is presiding over the family household at the time (Prov. 1:8-9; 2 Tim. 1:5; 3:15; 1 Tim. 5:10, 14; 1 Cor. 7:14).

REFLECTION

God's design is for fathers to lead, but when fathers are absent or unbelieving, God provides. Godly mothers and faithful caregivers can carry this work so the household still worships Him. Do we encourage every believing parent to take up this call?

Help for Fathers (or Mothers): Read *2 Timothy 1:5*. Ask: "What did Timothy learn from his mother and grandmother?" Remind children that God often works through faithful mothers to shape future leaders.

The Whole Counsel of God

175 **Q.** Over time, what part of Scripture should a family purpose to cover during family worship?

A. The whole counsel of God (Ps. 119:12-13, 171-172; 2 Tim. 1:4-5; 3:15-17).

REFLECTION

Over time, families should aim to cover the breadth of God's Word, not just favorite stories. Do we give our families the whole feast of Scripture, or only a few familiar bites?

Help for Parents: Read *2 Timothy 3:15–17*. Ask: "Why is all Scripture useful for us?" Make a simple reading plan to work through a whole book of the Bible together, or use one of the many Bible reading plans available.

Family Discussion

For Fathers to Ask at the Table

1. What is family worship, and why is it important for every household?
2. Who should lead family worship, and how does the Bible show examples of this?
3. What should families aim to cover over time when they worship together?

For Children (Simpler Prompts)

1. What is family worship?
2. Who should lead family worship at home?
3. What should we do when we worship God as a family?

Try This Tonight

Read *Deuteronomy 6:6–7* aloud. Ask: "What does it mean to talk about God's Word when we sit, walk, lie down, and rise up?" Then plan together one practical way to include Bible reading, prayer, or singing in your family's daily routine, beyond regular family worship. Close by praying that your family would love God's Word and worship Him faithfully.

Memory Verse

> *"As for me and my house, we will serve the Lord."—Joshua 24:15*

Hymn

"Break Thou the Bread of Life"

The Family and the Lord's Day

The Sabbath at Creation

176 **Q.** What is the origin of the Lord's Day?

A. The Sabbath was established by God at the close of creation week, when He blessed and set apart the seventh day as a day of rest (Gen. 2:1-3).

177 **Q.** Is the Sabbath uniquely connected to the Mosaic covenant?

A. No. The Sabbath was observed before the Mosaic covenant, being established at creation (Gen. 2:1-3; Exod. 16:22-26).

178 **Q.** Who is our perfect model for the Lord's Day?

A. God Himself, who personally rested on the first Sabbath day in history (Gen. 2:1-3).

REFLECTION

The Lord's Day is not man's idea but God's, established at creation. He Himself rested as our model. Do we see the Sabbath as a gift from our Creator, or as a burden?

Help for Parents: Read *Genesis 2:1–3*. Ask: "Why do you think God rested when He doesn't get tired?" Explain that God set a pattern for us to follow in worship and rest.

The Fourth Commandment

179 **Q.** What is the Fourth Commandment?

A. To remember the Sabbath day and keep it holy (Exod. 20:8-11; Deut. 5:12-15).

180 **Q.** How has God commanded us to do this?

A. We are to rest on this day, while laboring on the other six, as God demonstrated as a pattern during creation week (Gen. 2:1-3; Exod. 20:8-11).

REFLECTION

Remembering the Sabbath is not optional; it is one of the Ten Commandments. It teaches us to order our time with God at the center. Do our weekly routines show that God comes first?

Help for Parents: Read *Exodus 20:8–11*. Ask: "What does it mean to 'keep a day holy'?" Encourage children to think of one way they can prepare their hearts for the Lord's Day.

The Christian Sabbath

181 **Q.** How did the "Christian" Sabbath, also known as "the Lord's Day," begin?

A. Following Christ's resurrection, His disciples celebrated the Sabbath on the first day of the week, making this day the church's primary weekly gathering time for corporate worship (1 Cor. 16:1-2; Acts 20:7).

182 **Q.** What did the Apostle John call this day?

A. The Lord's Day (Rev. 1:10).

REFLECTION

With Christ's resurrection, the Sabbath became the Lord's Day, celebrated on the first day of the week. This reminds us of the new creation and eternal rest Christ secured. Do we rejoice in Sunday as resurrection day?

Help for Parents: Read *Acts 20:7*. Ask: "Why did the disciples gather on the first day of the week?" Share why Sunday worship is central for Christians.

The Family's Responsibility

183 **Q.** How does the Sabbath day, also known in the New Testament as "the Lord's Day," relate to families?

A. Parents are to ensure that all those under their care keep the Sabbath (Exod. 20:8-11; Deut. 5:12-14).

REFLECTION

Parents are called to ensure their whole household honors the Lord's Day. This is not only for individuals but for families together. Do we lead our homes to keep the Lord's Day?

Help for Parents: Read *Deuteronomy 5:12–14*. Ask: "Who in the household is called to rest?" Discuss how your family can make Sunday a true day of rest and worship.

The Spirit of the Day

184 **Q.** What spirit should accompany keeping the Lord's Day holy?

A. Rather than view the Lord's Day as a burden, families should embrace it as a day of delight, resting in God and joyfully worshiping with His people in the local church (Isa. 58:13-14; Ps. 22:22; 26:8; 40:9; 69:9; 84:1-2, 10; 122:1).

185 **Q.** What should fuel this joy for the Lord's Day?

A. A love for Christ and His church (Ps. 22:22; 26:8; 135:1-4; Heb. 10:24-25).

REFLECTION

The Lord's Day is not a burden but a delight. Families should rest joyfully, worship gladly, and love God's people in fellowship. Do we approach the Lord's Day with dread or with delight?

Help for Parents: Read *Isaiah 58:13–14*. Ask: "What does it mean to 'call the Sabbath a delight'?" Plan one way to make Sunday a joyful day (sharing a meal with believers, family singing, or an afternoon walk reflecting on God's goodness).

The Call to Gather

186 **Q.** Can weekly church participation take place remotely through the use of technology?

A. No. Corporate worship is a face-to-face affair where Christians lovingly build one another up in the faith, unless someone is suffering from prohibitive illness (Ps. 22:22; Heb. 10:24-25).

REFLECTION

Worship is not a private act but a gathering of God's people in person, face to face. Technology can serve as a supplement when sickness prevents attendance—but *never* a substitute for the church assembled. Do we treasure being with God's people enough to make worship together our weekly priority?

Help for Parents: Read *Hebrews 10:24–25*. Ask: "Why does God tell us not to neglect meeting together?" As a family, name three blessings you receive from being with your church body each Lord's Day.

The Body Needs Every Member

187 **Q.** What stands behind this call to gather together on the Lord's Day?

A. The church is one body with many members, and individual members need one another's personal company, unique giftings, and spiritual encouragement to thrive in the Lord (Eph. 4:11-16; 1 Cor. 12:12–31).

REFLECTION

The church is one body made up of many members, each with a God-given purpose. When we stay away, the body suffers. Do we come to church simply to receive, or also to build others up?

Help for Parents: Read *1 Corinthians 12:12–27*. Ask: "What happens to a body if one part stops working?" Discuss one way each family member can encourage or serve someone at church this week.

Families Together in Worship

188 **Q.** Is it appropriate for parents and their children to be separated during corporate church worship?

A. There is no biblical pattern for children being excluded from the corporate worship of God (Exod.

10:8-11; Deut. 12:6-7; 31:11-13; Josh. 8:35; Neh. 12:43; 2 Chron. 31:16-18; Ps. 148:12-13; Eph. 5:25-6:1-4; 1 John 2:12-14).

REFLECTION

God calls families to worship Him together. From the youngest to the oldest, all belong before His throne. Do our children see corporate worship as a family privilege, not a burden?

Help for Parents: Read *Deuteronomy 31:12–13*. Say: "God wants children to hear His Word and learn to fear Him." Talk about what your children remember from last Sunday's sermon or song.

Children and the Word

189 **Q.** Were young children separated from the reading of God's Word in Nehemiah 8:3?

A. It is unlikely, since neither children nor exclusion are mentioned in this text, which appears, instead, to reference half the children who spoke the language of Ashdod and could not understand the Hebrew language (Neh. 8:3; 13:24).

REFLECTION

Scripture gives no example of children being excluded from hearing God's Word. Even when understanding comes slowly, exposure to God's truth shapes tender hearts over time. Are we patient with our children as they learn to listen and grow in reverence?

Help for Parents: Read *Nehemiah 8:3, 13:24*. Explain simply: "Even children who didn't understand at first were taught to listen and learn." Encourage your children to listen for one truth they can remember each Sunday.

Flourishing in the Church

190 **Q.** What normally happens when Christian families faithfully commit to life in a biblically-ordered local church?

A. They will flourish and bear much fruit over time (Ps. 92:12-15).

REFLECTION

Families who plant themselves in the life of a faithful, biblical church will flourish. Consistency in gathering, serving, and worshiping together bears lasting fruit across generations. Is our family deeply rooted in the life of the church, or only loosely connected?

Help for Parents: Read *Psalm 92:12–15*. Say: "Those who are planted in God's house will flourish." Pray as a family for your church—its leaders, families, and future faithfulness.

Family Discussion

For Fathers to Ask at the Table

1. Where did the Lord's Day come from, and why is it still important today?
2. How did the day of worship shift from the seventh day to the first day of the week?
3. How can families make the Lord's Day a delight instead of a burden?

For Children (Simpler Prompts)

1. Who made the Sabbath day special?
2. What do we do on the Lord's Day?
3. Why should the Lord's Day be a happy day for families?

Try This Tonight

Read *Isaiah 58:13–14* aloud. Ask: "What does it mean to call the Sabbath a delight?" Then plan together one way your family can make the Lord's Day special—perhaps by preparing for worship the night before, having a special family meal, or spending extra time in Scripture and prayer. Close in prayer, thanking God for giving us a day of rest and worship.

Memory Verse

> *"I was glad when they said to me, 'Let us go into the house of the LORD.'"—Psalm 122:1*

Hymn

"Safely Through Another Week"

Grandparenting

The Crown of Old Age

191 **Q.** What does having grandchildren signify?

A. A mark of blessing from God (Ps. 128:5-6; Job 42:12-17; Gen. 48:11).

192 **Q.** How is the blessing of having grandchildren described?

A. As the crown of old men (Prov. 17:6).

REFLECTION

Scripture calls grandchildren "the crown of old men." Grandparenting is not a time to fade into the background but to shine with wisdom, love, and faith. Do we see grandparents as vital in God's covenant plan?

Help for Parents: Read *Psalm 128:5–6*. Ask: "Why are grandchildren called a blessing?" Share one way grandparents have been a gift to your family.

Grandparents Duties Toward Children

193 **Q.** What are the duties of grandparents toward their grandchildren?

A. There are many:

- They should have an earnest vision for them to know God and faithfully follow Him (Deut. 4:9; Ps. 71:17-18; 78:4-7);
- They should model genuine faith to them (2 Tim. 1:5);
- They should teach them diligently (Deut. 4:9; 6:1-2; 12:28; 2 Tim. 1:5, 3:15);
- They should praise God to them (Ps. 79:13; 145:4);
- They should recount God's righteousness to them (Gen. 18:19; Ps. 22:30-31; 145:4, 17);
- They should declare God's strength, power, and wonderful works to them (Ps. 71:17-18; 78:1-7);
- They should warn them of evil and protect them from it (Ps. 78:4-11; Jer. 2:9-11);
- They should be fruitful before them (Ps. 92:12-15);
- They should give them an inheritance (Prov. 13:22).

Children's Duties Toward Grandparents

194 **Q.** What are children's duties to grandparents?

A. At least two:

- Honor them with due reverence (Lev. 19:32; Rom. 13:7; 1 Tim. 5:1);
- Provide for them in old age, as necessary (1 Tim 5:4; Gen. 47:11-12).

REFLECTION

Children are called to honor and provide for grandparents in old age. Respecting the elderly is part of godly living. Do we treat older generations as burdens or as treasures?

Help for Parents: Read *Leviticus 19:32*. Ask: "How can we show honor to older people in our family and church?" Brainstorm one practical act of honor (like a visit, a letter, or an act of service).

Biblical Examples of Grandparenting

195 **Q.** What is the most poignant personal example of grandparenting found in Genesis?

A. That of Jacob, grandfather of Ephraim and Manasseh (Gen. 48:3-16).

196 **Q.** How did Jacob interact with his grandsons?

A. He kissed and hugged them and laid his hands on them and blessed them (Gen. 48:8-16).

197 **Q.** Who are some other examples of grandparents, both good and bad, found in Scripture?

A. There are many:

- Noah: Grandfather to Canaan (Gen. 9:25-26);
- Moses: Grandfather to Jonathan, a pagan priest (Judg. 18:30);[5]
- Naomi: Grandmother of Obed (Ruth 4:13-16);
- Eli: Grandfather to Ichabod (1 Sam. 4:15-22);
- Maachah: Grandmother of Asa (1 Kings 15:2, 9-13);[6]

---

5. The original Hebrew consonantal text (before vowel points or accents were added) indicates that Moses was Jonathan's grandfather. Later on, the Masoretes modified the text by inserting a suspended letter (nun) to change the reading from "Moses" to "Manasseh" to protect Moses' reputation. See: Michael Rydelnik and Edwin Blum, eds., *The Moody Handbook of Messianic Prophecy: Studies and Expositions of the Messiah in the Old Testament* (Chicago, IL: Moody Publishers, 2019), 63–64.

6. While some translations refer to Maachah as Asa's "mother," 1 Kings 15:2 shows her to be his grandmother.

- Athaliah: Grandmother of Joash (2 Kings 11:1-16; 2 Chron. 22:10-23:15);
- Lois: Grandmother of Timothy (2 Tim. 1:5; 3:15).

REFLECTION

Jacob blessed Ephraim and Manasseh with a holy kiss and laying on of hands. Lois, Timothy's grandmother, modeled sincere faith. Do we pray for and bless our grandchildren with this same intentionality?

Help for Parents: Read *2 Timothy 1:5*. Ask: "Why is Timothy's grandmother Lois remembered in Scripture?" Encourage your family to think of grandparents as carriers of a spiritual legacy.

Family Discussion

For Fathers to Ask at the Table

1. Why does the Bible describe grandchildren as "the crown of old men"?
2. What duties do grandparents have toward their grandchildren, and how are they different from parents' duties?
3. How should children and grandchildren honor

their grandparents?

For Children (Simpler Prompts)

1. What does the Bible call grandchildren?
2. How can you show love and respect to your grandparents?
3. What good things can grandparents teach us about God?

Try This Tonight

Read *Psalm 78:4–7* together. Talk about how God wants grandparents and parents to pass on His truth to future generations. If grandparents are nearby (or reachable by phone/video), have the children ask them to share one story of how God has helped them in their lives. Close by praying for grandparents and thanking God for the blessing of family across generations.

Memory Verse

> *"Grandchildren are the crown of the aged, and the glory of children is their fathers."—Proverbs 17:6 (ESV)*

Hymn

"Tell Me the Old, Old Story"

Death and Burial

The Priority of Burial

198 **Q.** What is one essential duty regarding property that families should pursue?

A. To secure a burial place for deceased family members (Gen. 23:3-20; 25:9-10; 35:29; 1 Sam 25:1).

199 **Q.** Why is a proper burial to be a priority for those who follow the God of Scripture?

A. Because it points to the sanctity of the body as created by God, and looks forward to the future bodily resurrection from the dead (Gen. 1:31; Deut. 34:5-6; Num. 20:1; Job 19:25-27; Matt. 27:57-60; Mark 6:27-29; Acts 8:2; 1 Cor. 15:42-49; 1 Thess. 4:13-18; Phil. 3:20-21).

REFLECTION

From Abraham to Christ, God's people have cared for the body in burial, showing respect for the body as His creation and hope in the resurrection to come. Burial proclaims that death is not the end.

Do we think of death with Christian hope, or do we avoid thinking about it at all?

Help for Parents: Read *Job 19:25–27*. Ask each family member: "What hope does this verse give you when you think about death?" Share briefly about Christ's resurrection as the guarantee of ours. Pray together, thanking God for the victory of Jesus over death.

Judgment and the Lack of Burial

200 **Q.** How does God's Word characterize those not given a proper burial?

A. As marked by God's judgment and curse (Deut. 28:26; 1 Kings 13:21-22; Jer. 16:3-6; 22:17-19; 29:22-23).

REFLECTION

Scripture speaks soberly about those denied burial—it is seen as a mark of God's judgment. This reminds us that death is not neutral: not only does how we live before God matter, but how we treat the bodies of dead loves ones. How does remembering this deepen our seriousness about sin and our gratitude for Christ?

Help for Parents: Read *Jeremiah 16:3–6*. Explain briefly that God sometimes withheld burial as a sign of judgment. Contrast this with believers' hope of being "sown in weakness, raised in power" (1 Cor. 15:42–43). Close with a short prayer of gratitude for Christ who bore judgment in our place.

The Question of Cremation

201 **Q.** Is cremation the way God wants us to treat the body of the deceased?

A. Nowhere in Scripture is cremation mentioned with approval (Amos 2:1; Josh. 7:15, 25; 1 Sam. 31:12-13; 2 Sam 21:12-14).

REFLECTION

While many cultures practice cremation, Scripture never commends it. Burial aligns with the biblical pattern of honoring the body and confessing resurrection hope. Do we view the body as God's creation, even after death, or merely as disposable remains?

Help for Parents: Read *1 Corinthians 15:42–49*. Discuss how burial pictures a seed being planted that God will raise in glory. If children are young, use a seed analogy: plant a seed in soil and talk about how something new and beautiful comes forth—just as God will raise His people at the last day.

Family Discussion

For Fathers to Ask at the Table

1. Why do you think God's people throughout Western Civilization cared so much about having a burial place for their families?
2. How does the way we treat the body after death show what we believe about the resurrection?
3. How can the hope of the resurrection comfort us when we think about death?

For Children (Simpler Prompts)

1. What happens to our bodies when we die?
2. Why do Christians bury the body in the ground?
3. Who promises to raise believers up again one day?

Try This Tonight

Read *1 Thessalonians 4:13–18* aloud. Then ask each person to share what part of this passage gives them the most hope. Close in prayer, thanking God that because Jesus rose from the dead, all who trust in Him will also rise in glory.

Memory Verse

> *"Jesus said to her, 'I am the resurrection and the life. He who believes in Me, though he may die, he shall live.'"—John 11:25*

Hymn

"I'll Fly Away"

Made in the USA
Coppell, TX
12 June 2026

81465414R10105